Hallowed Be Thy Names

Hallowed Be Thy Names

by

David Wilkerson

Rickfords Hill Publishing Ltd.

RICKFORDS HILL PUBLISHING LTD.
Perch Cottage, Halton Lane, Wendover. HP22 6AZ.
www.rhpbooks.co.uk

First Published 2001
This edition 2003
Second impression 2007
Third impression 2008

ISBN: 978-1-905044-09-2

Typeset by Avocet Typeset, Chilton, Aylesbury,
Buckinghamshire.

Cover design and print production for the publisher by
Bookprint Creative Services, <www.bookprint.co.uk>
Printed in Great Britain.

Contents

Introduction

Many books have been written about the various names of God. Most of these are scholarly works, exploring the deepest theological meanings behind each of God's names. They're exhaustive, covering the twenty-three compound names of God found in scripture, as well as the more than forty compound names of Jehovah.

In writing this book, Hallowed Be Thy Names, I have chosen not to cover every name of God. Nor have I sought to study every theological nuance of the names I cover. Rather, my purpose in exploring this subject has been to obtain a heart knowledge of God's names. I wanted to have a revelation of his names on a personal level – to appropriate their fullest meaning not for mere theological knowledge, but for my daily walk with him.

You see, each of God's names reveals a defining quality about our Lord's nature and character toward his people. And, as I searched the scriptures, I discovered that God revealed these names to his people only as they needed them – in their moments of deepest crisis. It dawned on me that this was how I wanted to learn my Lord's nature also – to know his heart toward us, his people, in our most desperate times. Therefore, I've chosen to explore in these pages the names of God that most relate to my own times of testing and crisis.

Simply put, this book is for every hurting believer who needs assurance and hope during his or her trying times. In my opinion, this includes every devoted servant of Jesus Christ. Scripture makes it abundantly clear that because of our commitment to the Lord, we're going to be put through the fire. And that's the very reason God revealed his names to his people in the first place – to bring them encouragement, hope and life. Likewise, I believe that at some point as you read this book, you'll find a special word of encouragement.

Why is it important for us to know these names of God? Here are just a few of the reasons the Bible gives us:

- The Psalmist says we receive God's deliverance through knowing his name. "Our help is in the name of the Lord, who made heaven and earth" (Psalm 124:8). "Because he has known my name ... I will deliver him" (91:15). "I found trouble and sorrow. Then called I upon the name of the Lord ... I was brought low, and he helped me" (116:3, 4, 6).
- Isaiah writes that we're kept by God when we trust in his name. "Who is among you that feareth the Lord, that obeyeth the voice of his servant, that walketh in darkness, and hath no light? Let him trust in the name of the Lord, and stay upon his God" (Isaiah 50:10).

In reality, God has only one name. In the Bible he calls himself the great I AM. "God said unto Moses, I AM THAT I AM: and he said, Thus shalt thou say unto the children of Israel, I AM hath sent me unto you" (Exodus 3:14).

What does the Lord mean by saying his name is I AM? He's telling us he's the everlasting one – the God with no beginning and no end. He always was, he is right now, and he always will be. And, as he explained to Moses, "I AM whatever you need, at any point in your life. That is my nature – to be for you whatever you need at any given time. My name is I AM – and I want my people to remember it."

Although I AM is God's only name, the ancient Hebrews used several other names to describe his nature and character. Often people have called these names "the names of God" – but, in reality, they're expressions of who our Lord is and what he's like.

It's important to note that although we may know someone's name, we may actually know very little about who that person is. This is true with God also. We can memorize all of the Lord's various names, and yet still know only the minimum of who he truly is. I believe this is why he revealed his names to Israel during their trials and crises. He wanted them to learn every facet of his loving nature toward them, especially as they faced difficult times.

Isn't this how our children get to know us? Whenever my four children relate to me, it's not only by my name. They relate to me by my nature and character – by the things they've learned about me through their experiences with me.

Hopefully, I've been a good father to them over the years – rejoicing over them in love, patient through their failures, available to them at all times, offering counsel, meeting their needs. And, as they've grown over the years, their knowledge of me in these ways has increased. Of course, certain basic things are implied with being a good father. One is to act as a protector and provider. Every caring father does his best to provide food, clothes and shelter for his children. Yet, providing these essentials is merely the basic duty of every father. Like any loving dad, I want to go beyond this in my relationship with my children. I want them to know me mostly by my caring heart toward them.

If someone were to ask my children, "Who's your father, and what's he like?", I would be grieved if all they could answer were the bare basics: "His name is David Wilkerson. He lives in New York City and pastors a church in Times Square. In my growing up years, he put a roof over my head and always put food on the table. He took care of me well."

This says nothing about my relationship with my children. Even if they were to add, "He's also a good father," it still wouldn't capture what I hope I am in my relationship to them.

Yet, sadly, this is all many Christians can say about their Lord. At times we're asked by non-believers, "You say you know God. Tell me – who is he, and what's he like?" Often, all some Christians can answer is, "He's the great I AM. He rules over heaven and earth, and he sits on his throne in glory."

But this says nothing about our heavenly father's relationship with us.

I believe our natural children get to know our nature and character toward them most especially during their times of crisis. When they're in the midst of pain, suffering and need, they recognize our deep care and provision for them. When my children were growing up, I didn't have to lecture them about what I'm like. I never had to say, "I'm your father – I'm patient, kind, full of mercy and loving kindness toward you. I'm tenderhearted over you, ready to forgive you at all times." It would have been ludicrous for me to make this kind of proclamation. Why? My kids learned about my love for them during their crisis experiences. And now, as they're grown and married with children of their own, my sons and daughters are getting to know me through a whole new set of experiences. They're learning even more about me by my attitudes and actions toward them in this new time of need in their lives.

So it is with us, in getting to know our heavenly father. From the time of Adam down through the cross of Christ, the Lord gave his people an ever-increasing revelation of his character. Yet he didn't do this simply by proclaiming who he is. He didn't try to reveal himself by merely announcing to Abraham or Moses, "The following names describe my nature: El Elyon, El Shaddai, El Olam, Jehovah Jireh, Jehovah Rophi, Jehovah Nissi, Jehovah Tsebaioth, Jehovah M'kaddesh, Jehovah Shalom, Jehovah Tsidkenu, Jehovah Makkeh, Jehovah

Shammah, etc. Now, go and learn these, and you'll discover who I am."

These Hebrew expressions do describe the wondrous glories and provisions that are wrapped up in our Lord's name. Yet God revealed these aspects of his nature to his people by actually doing for them what he proclaimed himself to be. He saw his children's need, foresaw the enemy's strategy against them, and intervened supernaturally on their behalf.

As you read this book, I urge you to get to know your heavenly father slowly, purposefully, on a heart level. You don't need to memorize all of these hallowed names in their Hebrew form. For example, instead of memorizing God's name as Jehovah Tsebaioth, simply learn him as the Lord of Hosts. Get to know the English meanings of his names well, and remember them.

I suggest you read only one chapter at a time. Keep this book on your night stand, and try a chapter each night. Then, when you're finished, go back over the chapters that have ministered to you in your trial. As you review those chapters, ask the Holy Ghost to recall to you the many facets of heavenly provision God has given you during your times of need. Then ask the Spirit to build into you a true heart knowledge of I AM – the God who is everything you need, at all times.

Pronunciation of the Names of God in this Book

El Elyon	El Ely-OWN'
El Shaddai	El Shad-DI'
Jehovah Jireh	Je-HO-va JI'-rah
Jehovah Rophi	Je-HO-va RO'-fee
Jehovah Makkeh	Je-HO-va MA'-keh
Jehovah Nissi	Je-HO-va NEE'-see
Jehovah Tsebaioth	Je-HO-va Se-baw-OT'
Jehovah Shalom	Je-HO-va Shaw-LOME'
Jehovah Tsidkenu	Je-HO-va Sid-KAY'-noo
Jehovah Shammah	Je-HO-va SHAW'-mah
Jehovah Rohi	Je-HO-va RO'-ee

1

El Elyon
El Shaddai
Jehovah Jireh

*"God Most High, Creator And Possessor of
Heaven and Earth"*
"God All-Powerful and All-Sufficient"
"The Lord Who Sees and Who Provides"

Genesis 14 describes the first war ever recorded in human history. A confederation of hostile kings declared war on Sodom and Gomorrah, and the two sides waged a battle in the "vale of Siddim." The hostile confederation won, and "the kings of Sodom and Gomorrah fled, and fell there; and they that remained fled to the mountain" (Genesis 14: 10).

The hostile confederation then set their sights on the vanquished cities of Sodom and Gomorrah. They invaded these cities, capturing the people and securing all their wealth and food supplies. "They took all the goods of Sodom and Gomorrah, and all their victuals, and went their way" (14:11). During this invasion, the hostile army took captive Lot, who was Abram's nephew: "They took Lot, Abram's brother's son, who dwelt in Sodom" (14:12).

Now, the Bible tells us Abram had 318 "trained servants" (14:14). This phrase indicates these men were practiced in the art of war. The servants evidently were trained to protect the interests of Abram's clan from plunder. And now Abram was determined to recover Lot and his family. So he led his servants in hot pursuit of the confederated army. When Abram and his militia had traveled some 140 miles, they finally overtook the invaders. They defeated the enemy soundly – a rout so lopsided, the fleeing confederate soldiers left behind all the spoils they'd stolen. Abram ended up rescuing all of the captives, including Lot, and recovering all of Sodom and Gomorrah's goods.

As we pick up the story, Abram and his men are heading back over a ridge in the valley just north of Jeru. What a sight Abram's caravan must have been. It was led by a bold man of God, followed by his troop of servant-soldiers, Lot and his family, the freed citizens of Sodom and Gomorrah, and all the treasures and food supplies taken by the confederate army.

As I picture this scene, I can't help wondering: Why did God allow Abram to save Sodom and Gomorrah? After all, God knew all along that they soon were to be judged. Why didn't he just let Abram rescue Lot and his family, and let the wicked Sodomites be taken captive?

My personal belief is that this was God's way of not allowing Satan to preempt his divine judgment. No doubt, the devil knew that God planned to destroy Sodom. In fact, Satan may have hoped the invaders' captivity of Sodom would help to spread these people's perverted lifestyle to other heathen nations. Then the devil would have had an army of demon-controlled missionaries spreading moral decay throughout the then known world.

But God stopped Satan in his tracks. He used Abram to bring back all the people of Sodom and Gomorrah to face his divine judgment. By doing so, God was quarantining them. Now he could burn out the disease from their vile society and stop its vicious spread.

We next see Abram in a scene that is vitally relevant to the church of Jesus Christ today.

On his victorious return from the battle, Abram was met by two kings – the king of Salem and the king of Sodom.

First, as Abram approached Jeru, the city's king came out to meet him. (Jeru was actually an early name of Jerusalem, the city of God. The word "Salem" was later added, meaning peaceful to form the name Jerusalem.) The king of Jeru was named Melchizedek, and the Bible refers to this mysterious figure in only three verses. Genesis 14:18 describes him as both "king of Salem" and "priest of the most high God." This dual description of king and priest alerts us to Melchizedek's role as a type of Christ. Indeed, Melchizedek's meeting with Abram was an amazing visitation. First, acting as priest, Melchizedek served Abram a covenant meal of bread and wine. Then, acting as king, Melchizedek accepted a tithe from Abram. Finally, Melchizedek is out of the picture, almost as quickly as he had flashed onto the scene.

This man obviously foreshadows the person and work of Jesus Christ. We see him referred to twice more in the scriptures. The first occurrence is 1,000 years after this scene, in Psalm 110: "Thou art a priest for ever after the order of Melchizedek" (110:4). Then, 1,000 years after that, Melchizedek is mentioned again, in Hebrews 7. This time the reference is to Jesus: "Thou art a priest for ever after the order of Melchisedek" (7:17).

Soon after his incredible meeting with Melchizedek, Abram was met by the king of Sodom. This same king had fled the battlefield as the marauding confederate army began winning. Afterward, when Abram came on the scene, the king had to sit by and watch as God's servant defeated the confederates. Now, as the king saw Abram returning in victory, he offered the godly man all the spoils of battle. The king told Abram, "Give me the persons, and take the goods to thyself" (Genesis 14:21).

To gain the full impact of the king's offer here, we need to examine the scene more closely. Here was godly Abram, leading home all the freed captives of Sodom and Gomorrah. Satan must have been enraged at the sight. His plan for spreading Sodom's wickedness had been demolished. Now he probably seethed, "This holy man has become the people's hero and deliverer. Worse, I just saw him communing with Melchizedek, the priest of God. The Lord must be planning to convert all of these Sodomites."

At that point, I believe, the devil filled Sodom's king with a spirit of jealousy. You can almost hear Satan's scheming voice speaking through this vile man: "Keep all the spoils, Abram. You can have everything we possess. Just give me back my people." In reality, the devil was pleading, "Please, Abram – take everything you want. Just don't take these souls away from me."

You have to understand – the goods that Sodom's king offered to Abram were more than just a wagon load of groceries. These were the spoils of two prosperous city-states. I am confident these spoils included great wealth: thousands of cattle, sheep, camels, donkeys, weapons, clothing, furnishings, treasures of gold, silver, diamonds, jewels and precious stones.

Yet just as quickly as the offer was made, Abram refused it without hesitation. He told the king, "I have lift up mine hand unto the Lord, the most high God, the possessor of heaven and earth, that I will not take from a thread even to a shoelatchet, and that I will not take any thing that is thine, lest thou shouldest say, I have made Abram rich" (Genesis 14:22-23). Abram was saying, in essence, "You can have the people and all the riches. *I'm taking Lot and his family with me.*"

**Sooner or later in our walk with Christ, we all
face these same two kings.**

At first, when we give our heart to Jesus, we win
a great battle. We defeat the powers of hell, robbing
Satan of the spoil he took from us when he ruled our
life. But afterward, as we're still glowing with spiritual victory and freedom, just down the road two
kings await us – the same two kings who awaited
Abram.

Abram faced as strong a temptation as any human
being ever experienced. Before him was an offer of
riches, material goods and fame. And Abram realized
he wouldn't be compromising his own reputation by
accepting it. But Abram didn't have to think twice
about his decision. His response to the king's offer
was a quick and clear no. Why? What mattered most
to Abram was preserving God's reputation, not his
own. In effect, he was telling the king of Sodom, "I'm
returning all of these things to you – the people, the
riches, everything. My Lord owns them all, anyway.
If he decides to make me wealthy, so be it. But I don't
want you to be able to brag that you made me rich."

Where did Abram get such detachment from this
world, such independence to be able to reject
outright the devil's offer of material blessing? How
did he obtain this tremendous authority, to be able
to say no to such a powerful temptation?

It's clear from scripture that Abram derived his
strength from a fresh revelation of who God is. You
see, Melchizedek had opened Abram's eyes to an
amazing   vision   of   God's   character: "He

[Melchizedek] blessed him, and said, Blessed be Abram of the most high God, possessor of heaven and earth: and blessed be the most high God, which hath delivered thine enemies into thy hand" (Genesis 14:19-20).

Embedded in this verse is a name for Jehovah God: El Elyon. It means, literally, "God most high, creator and possessor of heaven and earth." Melchizedek was declaring to Abram, "Your Lord is not just a God above all other gods. He's the creator of the entire universe. Everything in it belongs to him – all wealth, cattle, possessions. He's in control of everything you see around you."

This new name, El Elyon, provided Abram with a new discovery about the Lord. He had known God in one way, but not as Lord most high, creator and possessor of all things. Now Abram was convinced God had everything under control. That's why the patriarch immediately made an oath: "From now on, I'm going to trust only El Elyon to meet all my needs. If the Lord creates and possesses all things, then I won't accept a single shoelace from this Sodomite society. I don't want to depend on any man. Instead, I'm going to put my life, my family and my future totally into God's care."

Abram rejoiced over this marvelous discovery as he left his meeting with Melchizedek. And now, as he faced the king of Sodom, he had the power and faith to face any temptation. This is why Abram saw Sodom's goods as trivial. He scoffed at the king's offer, saying, "You offer me trinkets, Sodom, when my God owns the universe. He possesses the spoils of the whole earth. The Lord alone is my supply, all I will ever need. So, take your stuff and go. El Elyon has made me an offer I cannot refuse."

Abram's faith must have been totally rejuvenated at this point. I imagine him reasoning, "Lord, if you possess all that exists in heaven and earth, then possess me too. I want you to take control of my life – to rule over everything I am and everything I do." Of course, Abram did eventually become God-possessed. And at that point, his faith began to soar, increasing with every thought of the wondrous revelation God had given him.

Every devoted Christian has discovered the Lord as his saviour from sin. Yet have we also discovered him as El Elyon – God most high, creator and possessor of all things? Have we begun to see him with new eyes, as Abram did? Are we convinced he holds our entire lives and well-being in his hands?

Hebrews tells us our Lord never changes – that he is the same yesterday, today and forever (see Hebrews 13:8). Are you persuaded God is in absolute control over all things – all nations, all events, all circumstances in your own life? Are You able to face the storms, tests and trials in your walk, calmly testifying, "My God, El Elyon, has every-thing under control"? Do you trust his power to help you resist every temptation the devil throws at you? Can you trust that if God has created a new heart in you, he also has the power to create in you a hunger and thirst to know him more intimately?

We obtain this kind of power only by laying hold of the revelation that our God is El Elyon. In contemporary terms, this revelation means, "God is boss of everything. Therefore, there are no accidents in my life – no such things as fate, happenstance, good luck or bad. My every step is ordered by the Lord. Therefore, everything in my life – indeed, everything in this universe – is under his control. His word tells me Satan can't tempt me any more than I can bear. My boss is always faithful to show me the way of escape."

Abram used his fresh revelation to challenge the Lord.

Armed with his new discovery about God, Abram challenged the Lord: "Abram said, Behold, to me thou hast given no seed: and, lo, one born in my house is mine heir" (Genesis 15:3). It's as if Abram were saying, "Lord, I know you're El Elyon – creator and possessor of all things. So, where is my promised child? You said I would be the father of many nations. Yet here I am, still childless after all these years."

Years before, Abram had been confronted with another crisis, and his faith had begun to waver. You know the story: After years of trying, Abram's wife, Sarah, seemed unable to bear children. So she offered her handmaid, Hagar, to Abram to sire a son. At that point, Abram took matters into his own hands. He impregnated the handmaid, who bore a son, Ishmael.

Abram was eighty-six years old when Ishmael was born. He had hoped the boy would provide the seed God had promised. But in the Lord's eyes, this

child was illegitimate, because he was not the child
of faith and promise. The Lord told Abram, "This
shall not be thine heir; but he that shall come forth
out of thine own bowels shall be thine heir" (15:4).

Yet the Lord wanted to strengthen Abram's
wavering faith. So he entered into covenant with
Abram, making an oath to him that sealed his
promise of a seed. Still, nothing happened in the
years that followed. There was no sign that Sarah
would ever bear a child. And Abram was just getting
older. By the time Ishmael turned thirteen, Abram
was ninety-nine years old. This man had to be on the
verge of losing all hope that God's promise would
ever be fulfilled. Once again, his faith was being tried.

I believe scripture is making a point here to
everyone who has chosen to follow Jesus. It's saying
that God uses our crises – the most difficult, trying
times in our lives – to give us hopeful revelations of
who he is. Each revelation is like a separate beam
reflecting out of a diamond: It reveals a different
aspect of our Lord's nature, giving us fresh views of
his character and power toward us. These revelations beam especially brightly during our times of
crisis. God knows those are the most effective times
for him to reveal to us his ability and desire to
deliver us.

As Abram faced yet another crisis, the Lord
decided once again to give his servant a fresh revelation of himself. He wanted Abram to be fully
persuaded of his faithfulness. So, scripture says,
"When Abram was ninety years old and nine, the
Lord appeared to Abram, and said unto him, I am

the Almighty God; walk before me, and be thou perfect" (Genesis 17:1).

The Hebrew phrase for "Almighty God" here is El Shaddai. The literal meaning of this name is "God, all-powerful and all-sufficient." What an incredible revelation for Abram to receive at this time. God was speaking very personally to his servant here, saying, "Abram, you already know I have power over every condition in your life. I've convinced you that I'm in control of all things – that there are no accidents in your life, no situations that are merely fate or luck. I am the head, the chief, the boss of all creation – and my word is eternal. Now I'm going to tell you something else about my nature that you need to understand to continue in faith.

"I am not only in control of all things – but I also keep my word. No obstacle can keep my word from coming to pass. I'm not bound by the laws of nature or fettered by any man. I can do anything at any time. There are no mountains too high for me, no valleys too low, no rivers or oceans too wide. I'm supreme above the power of all nature, men and devils. When I say something is going to be done, it's already done. Nothing can stop my promise. I am El Shaddai – all-powerful, all-sufficient keeper of my promises. I guarantee my word."

God saw that Abram was focusing on all the impossibilities of his situation. Abram simply couldn't see past his age, his dried up body, Sarah's dead womb. So the Lord specifically revealed himself to Abram as the God who gives life to the dead. He opened Abram's eyes to the part of his nature that performs the impossible, that calls into existence things thought to be non-existent.

Once Abram received this revelation, he believed God was who he claimed to be. And afterward, Abram "was strong in faith, giving glory to God; and being fully persuaded that, what he had promised, he was able also to perform" (Romans 4:20-21). This godly man knew that God could not lie. And the Lord had sworn to make him a father of all nations. Surely, God would do what he said he would do.

Abram's newfound faith eventually brought forth the child Isaac, the promised seed. It also brought Abram his new name – Abraham, "father of a multitude." Now Abraham and his Lord were united in a special realm of faith. Moreover, Abraham had discovered the secret to walking uprightly before God.

May God help us to discover the secret that Abraham knew about walking uprightly before the Lord.

Here is the secret to a godly walk: we are to *receive* – to acknowledge, believe, embrace and act upon – the revelation God gives us of who he is. That's the secret, plain and simple. We are able to walk uprightly before the Lord – not because we have willpower, knowledge, or even a covenant promise in hand; we walk uprightly because we are fully persuaded that El Shaddai will keep his promises to us.

The evidence of such faith is rest of soul. Therefore, if your soul is not at rest, you are not in faith. Conversely, if you believe God is who he says he is – and that he's faithful to do what he has promised to do – then you don't have a worry in the world. You're confident all things work together for good to those who love the Lord and are called according to his purpose (see Romans 8:28). God has already promised he won't let the devil have you, nor allow anything to happen to you beyond what is common to every other human being (see 1 Corinthians 10:13). And, in the midst of every temptation, the Lord is always faithful to make a way of escape for you, so you're able to bear up under the pressure (see 1 Corinthians 10:13).

God gave Abraham the following covenant promise: "I am thy shield, and thy exceeding great reward" (Genesis 15: 1). This is known as the Abrahamic covenant. The Lord promised Abraham, "None of your enemies can harm you. I will always be faithful to deliver you, no matter what your circumstances. And I will personally be your reward. You are eternally mine, Abraham. And I'm going to maintain you, protect you and keep you for myself."

Why were these promises so important to Abraham? Let me remind you – this man lived in a very brutal and wicked society. His neighbours in the region of the lower Jordan led wild, evil, dissolute lives. God had declared that their "cup of iniquity" was filling up, and they would come under judgment. Yet, the Lord's assuring words

enabled Abraham to lead a holy life in the midst of
such abounding iniquity. How? Abraham believed
what God said: he was safe from all harm, because
the Lord was all-sufficient to keep his servant victorious over every evil of his day.

The same is true for us today. I'm convinced that
only by embracing the revelation of God's covenant
names are we able to lead godly lives. Have you
discovered your El Shaddai, God all-sufficient? It's
time for you to stop focusing on your own weaknesses, powerlessness and failures. Instead, believe
God's covenant promises to you. He has pledged to
keep you, teach you, put his fear in you, cause you
to walk in his ways, give you his Holy Spirit, blot
out all your sins and replace them with his loving
kindness. So, will you rest in his word – in the
biblical revelation of his names – that he will be
all-sufficient to you?

**In Genesis 22, we read about Abraham's
supreme test of obedience and faith.**

Abraham enjoyed a season of settledness with his
son of faith, Isaac. The boy's name means
"laughter," and indeed, this miracle child was the
joy of Abraham's old age. Yet, when Isaac was a
young man, the Lord called upon Abraham for a
supreme act of obedience. God told Abraham, "Take
now thy son, thine only son Isaac, whom thou
lovest, and get thee into the land of Moriah; and
offer him there for a burnt offering upon one of the
mountains which I will tell thee of" (Genesis 22:2).

When Abraham heard this word, he immediately began splitting wood to prepare for the trip. Then he gathered Isaac, two servants and a donkey, and set out for Mount Moriah. The mountain was some fifty or sixty miles away, and it would take the group about three days to get there.

You can be sure Abraham had plenty of time to think along the way. This had to be the most trying, anguished time of his life. In his mind, his son was already dead. Abraham himself was now nearly 130 years old, and Isaac was about 30. The patriarch had watched his son grow into manhood – laughing with him, clutching him to his bosom, teaching him the ways of the Lord. And now, after years of child-lessness and waiting for God's promise to be fulfilled, he was being asked to give up the one thing dearest to his heart.

God's instruction to Abraham had to be as confusing as it was anguishing. Abraham knew Isaac was the promised seed through whom nations would come. This was the son he and Sarah had waited to have for so long, the one who would provide the very lineage of the messiah. (We know Abraham was aware of this, because Jesus said, "Your father Abraham rejoiced to see my day; and he saw it, and was glad" [John 8: 56]).

Nevertheless, Abraham gave up his son in full faith. Think about it – he made the journey without once questioning God on the matter. Can you imagine the strength this required? We have to remember, Abraham was a human being just like us, with similar passions and weaknesses. Yet he made

a difficult decision to obey the Lord, based on blind
faith. And all the while, he was surrounded by
hostile, mocking heathen. Where did Abraham get
the faith to obey such a hard word?

It came directly from the revelation of God's
name. Abraham reminded himself, "My Lord has
told me he's the creator of all things. And I believe
him. So, even if I slay my son, I know God has the
power to raise him up. I'm convinced of his resurrection power." Hebrews confirms Abraham's
belief, telling us, "By faith Abraham, when he was
tried, offered up Isaac: and he that had received the
promises offered up his only begotten son …
accounting that God was able to raise him up, even
from the dead" (Hebrews 11:17-19).

When Abraham arrived at the foot of Mount
Moriah, he instructed his two servants to stay
behind while he and Isaac went to make sacrifice.
Even at this point, Abraham demonstrated great
faith. He told his servants, "I and the lad will go
yonder and worship, and come again to you"
(Genesis 22:5). He was telling them, "You'll see us
both go up the mountain – and you'll see us both
return."

Abraham made his way up the mountain,
carrying the sacrificial knife and the burning censer.
Isaac walked behind him, carrying the wood. At one
point, scripture says, "Isaac spake unto Abraham his
father, and said, My father: and he said, Here am I,
my son. And he said, Behold the fire and the wood:
but where is the lamb for a burnt offering? And
Abraham said, My son, God will provide himself a

lamb for a burnt offering: so they went both of them together" (22:7-8).

In many ways, this scene foreshadows the event of the cross. Isaac, the sacrificial son, carried wood up a hill, just as God's own son, Jesus, would do. And Abraham willingly offered up his son as a sacrifice for sin, just as the heavenly father would do. Moreover, during the three days' journey, Abraham considered his son as already being dead. Yet, when it was finished, Isaac emerged from the trip as if he'd been raised from the dead. Of course, this all prefigures the three days Jesus was dead before God raised him up.

You may wonder, "Why would the Lord demand a human sacrifice, when the Old Testament tells us he hated the practice? This was something the heathen did. Besides, the Bible later says obedience is better than sacrifice." The fact is, God was birthing a church, a nation of faith, through this event. And this whole scenario was crucial in telling every generation to follow that animal sacrifice could not atone for human sin. One day, there would have to be a human sacrifice, one that was holy and pure. And it would involve someone willing to lay down his life for all of humankind. Simply put, Abraham's journey was an illustrated sermon about the messiah. It pointed to the future sacrifice made by Jesus Christ for the sins of the world.

Our focus in this passage, however, is a new discovery that God gave to Abraham. What was this discovery? It was another great revelation of his name. In my opinion, this revelation is the key to further understanding the secret of an overcoming life.

When they finally arrived, Abraham prepared to slay his son. As he bound Isaac and laid him upon the altar, the son must have willingly obliged. After all, Isaac was an adult, and his elderly father never could have wrestled him down. For this reason, I believe Isaac acted in faith as well. His father had taught him the covenant as he grew up, and Isaac also had learned the revelation of God's names. Thus, Isaac must have believed in the Lord's all-sufficiency as well. Like his father, he knew that even if he died, God had the power to raise him up again. Yet even if God chose not to resurrect him, he would lay down his life anyway, in obedience to the Lord's command to Abraham. (This attitude also prefigured Christ, who willingly offered himself as the lamb to be sacrificed.)

What is the point of this scene for Christians who read it today? It is this:

Almost all new discoveries of God – all fresh revelations of his person, nature and character – are tied to some crisis, some intense human experience.

I stated earlier that we often discover more of our loving father's nature during our difficult times. It was during Sodom's crisis that God revealed himself to Abraham as El Elyon – God most high, creator and possessor of all things. Likewise, it was during Abraham's own crisis of doubt that God revealed his name as El Shaddai – God all-powerful and all-sufficient. Now God was leading Abraham into the greatest crisis any human being could ever experience – the sacrifice of his own child. Yet, out of this crisis, Abraham would receive the greatest revelation he could ever know about the heavenly father.

As the time neared for Abraham to raise the knife, he was already walking in mature faith. He could face this test of obedience now, because he trusted in the revelations God had given him. In each case, he had received God's word and mixed it with faith, taking its truth to heart. By this time, he had appropriated the power of each of God's names in his life. And now, as Abraham stood over his son, he was ready to obey God perfectly. He remembered the Lord's revelation of himself as El Elyon, creator of all things. Therefore, it would be a small matter for God to raise up Isaac from the dead. In addition, Abraham believed in El Shaddai – God all-sufficient, the one who keeps his word. The Lord had already assured him, "I have given you a son, Abraham. And you're going to see entire nations come out of him." It's clear that Abraham was acting on a faith founded solely on God's revealed promises.

Now this godly man lifted the knife. He was ready to thrust it through the heart of his beloved son. Then, suddenly, he was stopped by a voice from heaven: "And the angel of the Lord called unto him out of heaven, and said, Abraham, Abraham: and he said, Here am I. And he said, Lay not thine hand

upon the lad, neither do thou any thing unto him:
for now I know that thou fearest God, seeing thou
hast not withheld thy son, thine only son from me.
And Abraham lifted up his eyes, and looked, and
behold behind him a ram caught in a thicket by his
horns: and Abraham went and took the ram, and
offered him up for a burnt offering in the stead of his
son. And Abraham called the name of that place
Jehovah-jireh" (Genesis 22:11-14).

What an amazing miracle of provision. The whole
time that Abraham was preparing to slay his son,
God had a sacrificial animal ready nearby. The Lord
must have supernaturally put an appetite in that
ram, causing it to wander up the hillside. As the
animal rummaged for food, it got its horn stuck in a
bush.

Here was a glorious new discovery of God's
nature. He revealed himself to Abraham as Jehovah
Jireh – "the Lord who sees." In contemporary terms,
this phrase translates as, "God will see to it." It's a
name that speaks of provision.

We see this meaning illustrated in a later verse in
the same chapter: "And Bethuel begat Rebekah"
(22:23). Let me explain the connection here. At the
very moment Abraham was raising the knife over
Isaac, his brother Bethuel was raising the girl whom
God would eventually give to Isaac as a wife. It's as
if the Holy Spirit were telling Abraham, "Yes, I have
preserved the promise of your seed by saving your
son. Yet I also have provided for your seed. Your
brother has already given birth to the girl Isaac will
marry."

Isaac wouldn't meet Rebekah for another several years down the road. But this passage proves the nature of Jehovah Jireh, the provider: even before we call out to him, our God answers. Long before we're even born, he's at work forming and shaping the circumstances of our lives.

The name Jehovah Jireh also has another meaning: "God is showing us." In other words, our Lord will reveal to us everything we need to obey him. He'll see to it that we're provided with all the power, strength and resolve to do whatever he commands.

This last revelation of God's name has been greatly misinterpreted and distorted by some in the church.

I've known some men to point to their new car and smile, saying, "Jehovah Jireh." In short, they're declaring, "See what God provided for me." Yet, if you see Jehovah Jireh only as a supplier and provider of material things, then you don't have the true revelation of this glorious name. Our God is all of that, but he is much more besides. The apostle Paul echoes the full meaning of this name when he writes, "My God shall supply all your need according to his riches in glory *by Christ Jesus*" (Philippians 4:19, emphasis mine).

Our Lord promised to wipe away all our sins – and he did it. Jehovah Jireh saw to it that a substitute for sin was provided, through his son Jesus Christ. Likewise today, our Lord will see to it that the Holy Spirit provides us with all the power we need to obey his word. He has written these words above his every command: "Your God will see to it that you obey him. Jehovah Jireh will keep his promise to provide all faith and strength for you, through the power of the Holy Spirit."

You may wonder, "Even though God provided Abraham with the ram, did the outcome still depend on his faith? What if Abraham had hesitated to plunge the knife into his son? Would God's plan have been aborted then? What if Abraham had stopped and said, 'This is too much, Lord. I can't handle it'?"

God has no Plan B. That's why he told Abraham, "I want you to walk perfectly" – meaning, uprightly. Scripture is clear: when God gives a promise and swears to see it fulfilled, there can be no possibility of failure. Therefore, it wasn't possible for Abraham to fail. Why? God was going to supply his servant with any faith he needed (and, obviously, he supplied it). The God who revealed himself as "he who will see to it" made sure Abraham had everything he needed to obey his command.

God has made a covenant with us also. He said he'll cause us to obey him, and he'll endue us with all the power we need to walk uprightly before him. Because he has promised this, I believe he will do it. His very existence hinges on fulfilling these promises. It's as if he says, "I'm Jehovah Jireh. And if I don't keep my word – if I don't see to it that I fulfill what I say – my throne will collapse. I'll cease to exist, and the universe will dissolve. Everything will end."

The Bible states, "They that know thy name will put their trust in thee" (Psalm 9: 10). "The name of the Lord is a strong tower: the righteous runneth into it, and is safe" (Proverbs 18: 10).

The ancient Hebrews followed a practice of naming their sons with magnificently descriptive words. They believed that the good name they bestowed on their offspring actually endowed the child with the power to attain its qualities. God wants us to know that the same is true for us of his names. Every revelation is a different beam of his glory, each unfolding his love and provision for his children. And he wants us to run to the security of those names, fully persuaded of their meaning and power.

"For when God made promise to Abraham, because he could swear by no greater, he sware by himself, saying, Surely blessing I will bless thee, and multiplying I will multiply thee ... it was impossible for God to lie" (Hebrews 6:13-14, 18).

The Lord assures us, "I have committed all that I am to keep you by my grace."

2

Jehovah Rophi
Jehovah Makkeh
"The Lord Who Heals You"
"The Lord Who Smites"

At the Red Sea, Israel witnessed God's incredible destruction of the Egyptian army. The Israelites rejoiced in this victory, playing their instruments, dancing and singing, "The Lord ... hath triumphed gloriously: the horse and his rider hath he thrown into the sea" (Exodus 15:1).

Immediately after this miraculous deliverance, Israel began a journey into the desert toward the promised land. In three days, time, they covered some forty miles – yet they quickly realized they'd been going in circles. To their dismay, they had progressed only about twelve miles from where they'd started. To make matters worse, the Israelites "found no water" (15:22). After two days in the desert, the supply they'd brought with them was gone. In this brief amount of time, they descended from the heights of praise and ecstasy to the depths of despair.

Then someone spotted a body of water ahead. You

can imagine the wild foot race that took place to get to it. I can see the fastest and healthiest Israelites arriving first, quickly dunking their faces into the water, taking in big gulps. A few seconds later, however, they're spewing the water from their mouths. They cry, "This water is bitter, undrinkable. Don't swallow it – it's full of poison."

The people trailing behind them don't believe their claim. They also quickly drink in big gulps. But soon they're spewing out the bitter water too. Scripture says, "When they came to Marah, they could not drink of the waters of Marah, for they were bitter: therefore the name of it was called Marah" (15:23).

What did God's people do in this situation? "The people murmured against Moses, saying, What shall we drink?" (15:24). The very same people of God who had rejoiced in the Lord's glory just days earlier were now murmuring and complaining against him.

These people had seen God perform awesome miracles on their behalf in Egypt. First, the Lord supernaturally protected them, while all around them he devastated Egypt with plagues. Then, as Israel made their way toward the wilderness, God delivered them with the greatest miracle ever witnessed by man: the opening of the Red Sea – with giant waves piled high, held back by incredibly strong winds.

In my mind, God provided an even greater wonder. He removed all sense of reason from the Egyptian army. Who but a supernaturally blinded militia would rush in under such great walls of water? Any sensible soldier would have seen this wonder and thought, "Wait a minute – this is supernatural. Only God could do this. Everybody else can move ahead if they want to, but I'm not going anywhere." Yet the entire Egyptian army proceeded and was destroyed.

God's people had been absolutely defenseless against the powerful Egyptians. Yet they successfully escaped Egypt and survived without a single casualty. I ask you – how could any Israelite ever doubt God again, after witnessing such a miracle?

Here's how: As soon as the Israelites grew thirsty in the desert, they forgot all about God's awesome miracles on their behalf. It took them less than three days to begin to doubt him. The same is true of many Christians today. They once experienced miraculous wonders of God's delivering power. But now they doubt whether the Lord is on their side anymore. These people know nothing of their heavenly father's nature.

This is why so many believers rush all over the world looking for signs, miracles, deliverances. They're trying to get to know God through supernatural works and wonders. But nobody truly gets to know the Lord that way. The apostle Paul tells us in no uncertain terms that faith doesn't come through witnessing supernatural works or miracles, but through God's word: "Faith cometh by hearing, and hearing by the word of God" (Romans 10:17).

You may ask, "What is the specific word that produces faith?" It's the word that reveals who our heavenly father is. This is how we discover who he is – by seeing and believing for ourselves who he claims to be. And this occurs most often as God meets us in our trials.

So, you wonder, why did God lead the Israelites directly to the waters of bitterness at Marah? Why didn't he just take care of them, as he had at the Red Sea? In that situation, he took control of an entire sea of water for them. So, obviously, he could have easily changed the waters at Marah as well. All he had to do was speak a word, and those waters would have been purified before the Israelites ever arrived. Why didn't he do that?

The Lord had brought his people to Marah in order to deal with them. He was about to begin building his wilderness church. But he couldn't begin that work because the camp was filled with a deadly disease, infecting virtually everyone. What was this disease? The Hebrew root word for Marah means "corruption of bitterness." A spirit of bitterness had spread throughout Israel, and it had to be dealt with.

I've often wondered how the Israelites became so bitter in the first place. In my opinion, something happened back in Egypt that had caused them to grow bitter. Now the roots of that bitterness were alive, and they exploded at the waters of Marah. The Lord simply couldn't lead his people another step unless this deadly disease was dealt with. So, the first place he took them in the wilderness was to this pool of bitterness. Why? He wanted to use the bitter waters of Marah as a mirror to hold up to the people's hearts. As they looked into the poisonous pool, they would see a reflection of their own embittered souls.

Try to picture the scene at Marah, as the people spewed out the bitter water. They must have been utterly confused. I imagine them gathering in groups within their clans, trying to figure out why God's blessing and favour had disappeared from them so quickly. They may even have tried to worship the Lord, but they probably couldn't muster up the spirit to do it. They were unable to quench their thirst, physically or spiritually, no matter how hard they tried.

Please note – this is exactly what bitterness does to people. It brings on confusion, a sense of God's disfavour, and an inability to worship. In my opinion, that is the message behind this story about Israel. I believe God is using a former generation of his people as an illustrated sermon to us. He's trying to warn us about the deadly disease and consequences of an embittered heart.

I've concluded that most bitterness among believers can be traced back to a disappointment with God.

Almost every time I talk with a Christian who's bitter, that person has experienced a deep disappointment with the Lord. Perhaps this describes your life. Maybe your bitterness goes back to a time of crisis – marriage problems, family upheaval, a financial struggle, a tragic illness slowly draining the life of a loved one. You were in need, hurting, crying out to God for help, believing for a miracle, doing the best you knew how. But the Lord didn't seem to be there for you. Your trial dragged on, and over time things just got worse.

After a while you began to wonder, "How could God allow this to go on? I've loved him, believed him, prayed to him. But nothing seems to change." You didn't dare allow yourself to get angry at the Lord. And you made sure you didn't do anything to cut yourself off from him. But deep down, you were disappointed. And soon, a seed of bitterness took root in your heart. Over time that root sprang up and blossomed. Now it continues to grow and spread in your soul.

Childhood wounds can fester into roots of bitterness. Certain traumas – abuse, beatings, molestation, abandonment – all leave their marks deep inside. And they often leave a trail of bitterness and unforgiveness in their victims' lives.

For example, I'm amazed by the number of letters our ministry receives from wives who say their believing husbands hate the Christmas holiday. Many of these men were traumatized somehow by an awful childhood experience. And now they're moody, irritable, even hateful when the holidays come around.

One woman writes that her husband mocks her gift-giving. He won't let her put up even a Christmas wreath. She traces his bitterness back to an experience he had with his alcoholic father as a boy. One Christmas the only present he received was a broken toy his drunken dad had pulled from a garbage can. While all of this boy's friends were showing off their toys outside, he was too embarrassed to leave the house. The experience left a deep mark on him, and he never got over it. Now he hates Christmas.

I believe the "corruption of bitterness" in Israel began in Egypt, when their hopes were so high after God sent Moses to them.

When Moses arrived on the scene, suddenly the Israelites' hopes were renewed. Here was a man who claimed to be sent by the Lord. And he backed up his claims by working supernatural signs and wonders.

To fully grasp the impact Moses' presence had on Israel, we have to understand these people's circumstances. They'd spent years in bondage, enslaved in the iron furnace of Egypt. Now, as Moses appeared, bringing signs of great hope, "The people believed: and when they heard that the Lord had visited the children of Israel, and that he had looked upon their affliction, then they bowed their heads and worshipped" (Exodus 4:31).

But Israel wasn't delivered right away. In fact, the people saw their plight grow even worse. The Egyptian taskmasters' whips came down on their backs harder than before. And Pharaoh decided he would no longer supply them with the straw they needed to meet the quota of bricks he demanded of them. Even worse, he increased their quotas.

You can imagine the Israelites' total disappointment, both with God and with Moses. The Bible tells us, "They met Moses and Aaron, who stood in the way, as they came forth from Pharaoh: and they said unto them, The Lord look upon you, and judge; because ye have made our savour to be abhorred in the eyes of Pharaoh, and in the eyes of his servants, to put a sword in their hand to slay us" (5:20-21).

I must confess, I've had little patience over the years with Christians who've harboured bitterness. At times, I've preached hellfire-and-brimstone sermons against their debilitating sin. And I did so with good reason: I've seen deeply rooted bitterness end up causing heart attacks, crippling diseases, depression. I could never understand why the embittered people I preached to didn't recognize what their bitter condition was doing to them.

Now, years later, I am awestruck as I see how tenderly the Lord dealt with the murmuring, complaining, bitter Israelites. God's gentle love toward his people, in spite of their awful condition, simply melts my heart. I am moved to ask God to give me his great love for those children of his who are burdened down with bitterness.

Here is what I found most amazing about this passage: The Lord could have wiped out Israel at Marah. God had given these people incredible, undeniable miracles of deliverance. Yet, ever since their experience in the furnace of Egypt – all through the supernatural plagues and the miraculous parting of the Red Sea – the Israelites continued to cling to doubt, fear and unbelief. First, they didn't

believe Moses, the Lord's servant. Then they
constantly questioned whether God was with them,
behaving at every turn as if he'd forsaken them.

The Israelites' deep disappointment with the Lord
was symbolized by the tiny golden idols they hid in
their tents. These people had carried their idols with
them through every mighty miracle of deliverance.
So, what did God do about their idolatry? Did he
chastise them or threaten to wipe them out? No, not
at this time. Instead, he responded by giving his
people a fresh revelation of his loving nature toward
them. When they got to Marah, God directed Moses
to cut down a tree and cast it into the bitter waters.
Then, scripture says, "When he had cast [it] into the
waters, the waters were made sweet" (Exodus
15:25).

Once again, we could digress briefly into the
subject of another healing tree – the one that appears
later, at Golgotha. Jesus cast that tree – the cross of
Calvary – into the bitter depths of all our sins, sweet-
ening the waters of life for us. But for now, I want to
stay focused on the subject at hand – the important
revelation God gave to Israel about his nature.

**We see once more that our God comes to us in
our crises and failures, bringing us into a new
discovery of who he is and giving us another
revelation of his loving kindness.**

It is at Marah that we discover Jehovah Rophi –
"the Lord who heals you." The root word for heal
here means to fix or mend. God told Israel, "If thou

wilt diligently hearken to the voice of the Lord thy God, and wilt do that which is right in his sight, and wilt give ear to his commandments, and keep all his statutes, I will put none of these diseases upon thee, which I have brought upon the Egyptians: for I am the Lord that healeth thee" (Exodus 15:26).

This is the passage that convicted me and broke my heart. The Lord is telling his people here, "I'm a God who wants to heal your diseases. I'm not inclined to cast you aside. My heart is to mend you completely – body, soul and spirit. I want you to know this about my character toward you – that I'm your healer."

So, reader, what do you need to be healed of? Maybe you're bitter at God for allowing your trial to continue. Or, perhaps you're angry at society or certain individuals. You may have an unforgiving spirit toward someone who has hurt you. You've convinced yourself, I can't forgive that person. I don't care how many scriptures you quote to me, I'm not even going to try to forgive him. You don't know what I've been through because of what he did to me. I'll leave it to God to deal with him. I'm taking this to my grave." (Yes, you surely will take it to your grave. In fact, it will be attached to you as you stand before the judgment seat of Christ – because, despite Jesus' clear command, you refused to let go of your bitterness.)

I ask you: What is the more important healing to receive – physical or spiritual? I can't help wondering what purpose there is in being healed of bodily sickness – diabetes, cancer, heart disease – if we're not supernaturally healed of our bitterness, resentment and pride. After all, these branches all come from the same tree.

It doesn't matter what your condition is. God says his nature is not to cut you off. He's telling you, "Yes, I'm Jehovah God, high and holy. But I'm also Jehovah Rophi, and I want to heal and mend you. I know you're mad at me. Your heart has been full of bitterness toward me for a long time. You don't want to voice it, but deep down you think, 'Why did God allow this to happen to me?'

"I want you to realize, I know where your bitterness comes from. And I'm coming to you now in your bitter condition. You've said you can't let go of your bitterness. And now you see it bringing strife into your life. It's ruining your marriage, your family. I want to pluck that bitterness out of you and heal you, so you don't have to carry it another day. Then I want you to enter back into all the peace and joy I desire for you.

"Right now, I'm revealing something more to you about my nature. I'm Jehovah Rophi, your healer and mender. And my heart is absolutely inclined to resolve your problem of bitterness. I want you back in my loving arms, full of my comfort."

Even if you harbour bitterness in your heart, you're still the Lord's possession. And he's offering you total healing. He has revealed himself to you as Jehovah Rophi – your healer and mender – and he's waiting for you to trust him. He longs to restore you to a clear conscience, to good physical health, to his divine peace and favour. And he stands waiting for you now, wanting to forgive you, cleanse you and give you a new heart. Your physical healing is included, but the healing of your spirit must come first.

There is a willful rejection – a stubborn holding onto hatred and unforgiveness – that provokes God's fiery indignation.

I've known many bitter Christians who refused to seek God's help. They rejected his offer of healing, as if he couldn't understand their hurt or pain. This is a very serious matter. These believers don't realize that they've turned down their only possible cure. As a result, their bitterness grips them so tightly that it takes over their lives. Suddenly, it has become an idol in their hearts. Now it's their reason for living, the very focus of their existence. It's all they can think or talk about. And it has begun to alienate them from their family and friends.

"Looking diligently lest any man fail of the grace of God; lest any root of bitterness springing up trouble you, and thereby many be defiled" (Hebrews 12:15). The Greek word for defiled here means contaminated. If you hold onto your bitterness, it will contaminate your family, your children, your co-workers. Whatever you touch will become infected by your bitter spirit.

Scripture warns us not to reject God's offer of healing: "If we sin willfully after that we have received the knowledge of the truth, there remaineth no more sacrifice for sins, but a certain fearful looking for of judgment and fiery indignation, which shall devour the adversaries" (10:26-27). In other words, we have received the knowledge of Jehovah Rophi. And if we reject his offer of healing, we have to face his fiery indignation. In simple terms, we could lose our eternal soul by rejecting his healing and grace and continuing in stubborn bitterness.

Listen to this powerful warning: "Follow peace with all men, and holiness, without which no man shall see the Lord" (12:14). God's word makes it clear: If you refuse to make peace with someone by holding onto bitterness against that person, you have no chance of seeing the Lord – none.

Bitterness brings about a terrible crisis.

If you hold onto bitterness, there finally comes a time when God has to quarantine you. Of course, he still loves you, but he can't allow your virus to contaminate his godly ones around you.

The Lord uses this kind of crisis to reveal something else about his nature: he is Jehovah Makkeh, "the God who smites." He says in Ezekiel, "I will recompense thee according to thy ways and thine abominations that are in the midst of thee; and ye shall know that I am the Lord that smiteth" (Ezekiel 7:9).

You may wonder, "My Lord is a smiting God? Where's the grace in that?" I tell you, this aspect of God's nature is all about grace. In the book of Proverbs, God advises every parent to use the rod to chasten their foolish, disobedient children. This discipline is meant to awaken them, recover them and lead them back to wisdom. Likewise, God himself smites his own rebellious children to return them to his holy ways. "Foolishness is bound in the heart of a child; but the rod of correction shall drive it far from him" (Proverbs 22:15).

Jehovah Makkeh says to us, "I've got to discipline you in order to correct your ways. Otherwise, you're headed for tragedy. If you hold onto your bitterness, your life will start to unravel. Everything will go wrong. You'll descend into utter confusion. Your home life will become chaotic. All your relationships will begin to sour, and you'll think everyone is against you – your family, your friends, your co-workers. You'll end up losing everything."

Our Lord doesn't want to lose any of his children. And when we turn down this wonderful offer from Jehovah Rophi, there remains no other way to healing. That's when he becomes to us Jehovah Makkeh, the God who smites. This is the aspect of his nature that refuses to let us go. He says, "I can't allow your bitterness to continue. The time has come for it to end now. I've come to you in love, mercy and great compassion. Yet you've rejected my offer, time after time. Now I have to apply the rod to you. There has to be a smiting."

God revealed this aspect of his character to Israel after they ignored his many merciful warnings. In great love and compassion, the Lord had sent his prophets and servants to them, warning that if they continued to reject his calls to obedience, he would

bring down his wrath: "They shall know that I am
the Lord, and that I have not said in vain that I
would do this evil unto them" (Ezekiel 6:10). "The
rod hath blossomed, pride hath budded" (7:10). God
was telling them, "Your bitterness has now taken
dominion in your lives. It has blossomed into pride.
And that's going to lead you to destruction."

God eventually smote Israel by sending them into
captivity. He took away their joy and peace and
brought shame and confusion upon them, unsettl-
ing their lives. Yet, the whole time, he was after one
thing – repentance. His desire was to pardon and
restore his beloved people.

"Now will I bring again the captivity of Jacob, and
have mercy upon the whole house of Israel, and will
be jealous for my holy name; after that they have
borne their shame, and all their trespasses whereby
they have trespassed against me, when they dwelt
safely in their land, and none made them afraid.
When I have brought them again from the people,
and gathered them out of their enemies' lands, and
am sanctified in them in the sight of many nations;
then shall they know that I am the Lord their God,
which caused them to be led into captivity among
the heathen" (Ezekiel 39:25-28). God was saying, in
essence, "When you know me as Jehovah Makkeh –
the God who smites to heal – then you'll know deliverance, victory and restoration. I'll smite you with
discipline, to drive out all your deadly rebellion."

Until you allow Jehovah Rophi to heal your bitterness, you can't go a step farther. If God were to heal
you of some physical illness without healing the

disease in your soul, he would be blessing and condoning your sin. And he would be providing you with new strength to indulge your bitterness. That's why he beseeches you now: "I want to heal you, not to smite you. Call upon me, yield to my Spirit – and I'll set you free. If you don't, you'll know me as Jehovah Makkeh, the God who smites. I love you, and I want you to choose healing."

If you reject God's glorious revelation as your healer – if you scoff at his offer, refusing to be mended – you'll be given over to your sin. And, like Korah in the Old Testament, you'll cause your family to be swallowed up in destruction.

It's time for you to turn to Jehovah Rophi. Get the process started by praying, "Lord, I've carried this bitterness for too long. Now I know it's time for me to be delivered. I want to be free." He'll take it the rest of the way. His Holy Spirit will bring you into a peace you've never known, causing you to sing, dance and shout. You'll sleep as you haven't slept in ages, because you'll be back in God's favour. And he'll begin to work new things in your life, bringing you renewed hope – because you choose to know him as Jehovah Rophi.

He's calling you to repent of your bitterness, today. He longs and yearns to heal your hurting soul. Give it to him.

3

Jehovah Nissi
"The Lord Our Banner"

Amalek was the first nation to declare war on Israel. In turn, Amalek was the first nation God declared war on. Exodus describes the Lord's declaration against Amalek in the following scene:

"Then came Amalek, and fought with Israel in Rephidim. And Moses said unto Joshua, Choose us out men, and go out, fight with Amalek: tomorrow I will stand on the top of the hill with the rod of God in mine hand. So Joshua did as Moses had said to him, and fought with Amalek: and Moses, Aaron, and Hur went up to the top of the hill. And it came to pass, when Moses held up his hand, that Israel prevailed: and when he let down his hand, Amalek prevailed. But Moses' hands were heavy; and they took a stone, and put it under him, and he sat thereon; and Aaron and Hur stayed up his hands, the one on the one side, and the other on the other side; and his hands were steady until the going down of the sun. And Joshua discomfited Amalek and his people with the edge of the sword. And the Lord said unto Moses, Write this for a memorial in a book, and rehearse it in the ears of Joshua: for I will utterly put out the remembrance of Amalek from under heaven. And Moses built an altar, and called the name of it Jehovah-nissi: for he said, Because the Lord hath sworn that the Lord will have war with Amalek from generation to generation" (Exodus 17:8-16).

Two verses in this passage grab my attention. Both appear toward the end of the passage: *"The Lord said unto Moses ... I will utterly put out the remembrance of Amalek from under heaven ... the Lord hath sworn that the Lord will have war with Amalek from generation to generation"* (17:14,16).

As I reread this particular passage recently, it took me a while to accept what God was saying. The Lord was declaring permanent war on a particular nation.

My question now is, who was this nation of Amalek? What was there about these people that caused the God of the universe to go on record as stating, in essence, "I'm going to do battle against you from generation to generation. And I'm going to make sure you're utterly destroyed, so that your memory is erased from history"?

This declaration tells us something very important about Israel's skirmish with Amalek at Rephidim. Obviously, the conflict had to do with more than just a local physical battle. It involved more than Moses standing on a hill with his arms lifted up while Joshua led Israel's troops in combat. We're told that Israel won this particular battle – but as we read more about this enemy, Amalek, it becomes clear there is more to the passage than meets the eye. Indeed, Israel's war with Amalek would rage on for centuries.

I believe Israel's ongoing conflict with Amalek represents a spiritual war still being fought today. This war involves every Christian. You see, Amalek is a type of the devil's hostility toward Christ and his body on earth. The margin note in an old Puritan Bible states the following as God's reason for declaring war on Amalek: "because his hand is against the throne of God." This ongoing war continues because Satan has never ceased his efforts to thwart God's eternal purposes.

It's helpful for us to examine exactly who the Amalekites were. They were descendants of Amalek – the grandson of Esau, Jacob's twin brother. We know Esau as the man who despised the holy things of God by selling his birthright for a mere pot of soup (see Genesis 25:34). The Bible says God despised Esau because of his wickedness: "I hated Esau, and laid his mountains and his heritage waste for the dragons of the wilderness … They shall build, but I will throw down; and they shall call them, The border of wickedness, and, The people against whom the Lord hath indignation for ever" (Malachi 1:3-4).

As we read of God's hatred for these nations, we need to keep in mind that the Lord has always been full of grace and mercy. Scripture tells us he is the same yesterday, today and forever – that his nature and character never change. Therefore, God was as merciful in the Old Testament as he is in the New.

Our Lord is, and always has been, a God of love and mercy. However, he states very clearly here: "My indignation will burn against these nations forever."

What exactly is happening here? It's clear to me that God is speaking of none other than Satan and his demonic powers. Amalek represents the devil – the enemy of the Lord, whose "hand was against the throne of God." Continuing up to Jesus' lifetime, Satan "put his hand against God's throne" by trying to destroy the seed that would bring forth the promised Christ. The enemy did everything he possibly could to wipe out God's people.

Make no mistake, Satan knew exactly what God's promised seed was all about. He was in the garden of Eden, listening as God told Adam that a seed would come forth to crush the serpent's head. The devil also was present on Mount Moriah, when Jehovah Jireh provided a ram to replace Isaac as the sacrificial offering. Satan knew this animal represented Jesus, the sacrificial lamb. And he was fully aware of what God meant when he told Abraham that all humankind would be blessed by his seed. That's why Satan declared war on God's throne. He was determined to do battle against the Lord's eternal purposes concerning this coming messiah.

Who but Satan himself could have possessed Pharaoh? This evil man was clearly devil-directed. He decreed that every male child in Israel was to be cast into the river and drowned. Obviously, Pharaoh was the mouthpiece and earthly power for a demonic spirit that was determined to kill off the promised seed.

At present, Satan's warfare continues against God's seed, the church of Jesus Christ. The devil is out to destroy all who would inherit eternal life through the promise of the messiah. That's why he has aimed his weapons at everyone who calls himself after Jesus' name.

Scripture suggests that this war God declared against Amalek is an everlasting conflict. And here, in Exodus 17, the enemy was readying himself to engage in another attack. Satan saw Israel headed for Canaan, the promised land where God would settle his people. The devil knew the prophecies concerning this land. He was fully aware that this physical, geographical nation of Israel would be the place of rest from which the seed would come. He knew a lineage would emerge from it – a mother, then a grandmother, then a great-grandmother, and so on, until finally a descended daughter would give birth to the Christ child. Now the devil was determined to do everything in his power to stop this prophecy from coming to pass.

The spirit of Satan instigated and waged war on Israel for one purpose – to annihilate the seed of Abraham through which his own destroyer would come.

The devil was not warring against Israel, but against God himself. As has been stated, "His hand was against the throne of God." Satan was never after the Jew, but after the Christ whom the Jewish nation would give birth to. Therefore, this was much more than a flesh-and-blood war; it was a war between heaven and hell. That's why we see God's people facing war after war with Amalek in scripture. Amalek was a Satan-controlled nation of people. And this war was a perpetual conflict waged against God by the principalities and powers of hell.

Exodus 14 is not the last we hear of the Amalekites. We see them next in Numbers 14. At that point, God told Israel to return to the wilderness. He refused to lead them into the promised land because of their continual sin of unbelief. He told the Israelites in no uncertain terms, "I'm not going with you anymore. I'll take your children into the land of promise, but you're not going in. You're going back to the wilderness, where you'll experience another thirty-nine years of despair." Then, scripture says, "The Amalekites came down ... and smote them, and discomfited them" (Numbers 14:45).

The Amalekites just kept rising up. We hear of them again four hundred years later, when Saul was king over Israel. God gave Saul specific instructions through the prophet Samuel, "Now go and smite Amalek, and utterly destroy all that they have, and spare them not; but slay both man and woman, infant and suckling, ox and sheep, camel and ass" (1 Samuel 15:3). God was telling Saul, "I want you to kill every man, woman and child of Amalek. And I want you to destroy all the spoils you take. Amalek is the sworn enemy of God, the one set on destroying the seed. You must wipe them out completely."

Saul won the skirmish against Amalek. But, in direct disobedience to God's command, he spared King Agag and kept the best spoils from battle. When Samuel saw what Saul had done, he was grieved beyond words. The prophet took matters into his own hands, personally picking up a sword and hacking King Agag to death. Yet even after this smiting, a remnant of Amalek would survive and rise up once again.

Later, the book of First Samuel describes an Amalekite attack on David. While David and his men were out doing battle, the Amalekites invaded their home village of Ziklag. The enemy raiders burned the town to the ground, took all the goods and kidnapped their families. When David and his men returned and saw what had happened, they pursued the Amalekites and overtook them. They won that battle, recovering their families and everything that had been stolen from them. But once again, four hundred young Amalekite men escaped.

Years later, during Hezekiah's reign, God's promise to wipe out Amalek was finally fulfilled. The Bible says the sons of Simeon waged war against the Amalekites, "and they smote the rest of the Amalekites that were escaped" (1 Chronicles 4:43). This was the literal fulfillment of Moses' prophecy. Now, as a nation, Amalek was destroyed. Only an insignificant remnant was left.

Yet the spirit that possessed the Amalekites continued to torment God's people. Even though Amalek had few surviving descendants, an Amalekite spirit had spread around the world. We see this demonstrated several generations later when Haman, a devil-possessed man, rose to power and plotted to wipe out Israel completely.

Here's an amazing fact about this story: Haman was an Amalekite, a distant descendent of an Amalekite king named Agag. (All of the Amalekite kings took the name Agag. The name represented an office, the way the title of Pharaoh represented the leader's role in Egypt.) Scripture calls Haman "the Jews' enemy" (Esther 3:10). Using subtle devices, this evil man seduced a pagan king into signing the Jews' death warrant. Scripture says, "The letters were sent by posts into all the king's provinces, to destroy, to kill, and to cause to perish, all Jews, both young and old, little children and women, in one day" (3:13).

I ask you – does this sound like the mad crusade of a single Jew-hater, a descendant of the remnant of the Amalekites? Was Haman personally going to take revenge on an entire race of people because, as this story tells us, one Jew, Mordecai, would not bow to him? No – this was the same, age-old spiritual conflict. It was a war against God's throne – an attempt to abort a coming Saviour who would deliver God's people from Satan's power. I tell you, Haman was merely an instrument the devil was using to try to accomplish his plan. The satanic spirit of Amalek that possessed this man was now declaring, "I'm going to kill off every Jewish man, woman and child. I'll wipe them off the face of the earth entirely. Then there won't be any chance of a messiah coming to destroy me."

But God had his own human instrument in place to crush Satan's plan. He raised up a single person among that generation, a young woman named Esther, to accomplish his eternal purpose. Esther was the niece of Mordecai, the Jew who refused to bow to pagan royalty. This godly young woman instructed every Jew in the land to fast and pray for three days. You know the rest of the story: the Lord gave Esther the king's ear, and Haman's diabolical plan was exposed. The devil suffered a great defeat in this battle. Not one Jew was killed – and Haman ended up hung on the very gallows he'd built to execute Mordecai.

Let's focus again on the battle at Rephidim.

Now we return to Rephidim, to the battle between Israel and the Amalekites. May God open our spiritual eyes to see what the Holy Spirit would teach us here about our own spiritual warfare today. And I believe the lesson is urgent. Peter reminds us, "Your adversary the devil, as a roaring lion, walketh about, seeking whom he may devour" (1 Peter 5:8). Likewise, Paul tells us, "Now all these things happened unto them for ensamples: and they are written for our admonition, upon whom the ends of the world are come" (1 Corinthians 10:11). "Now these things were our examples, to the intent we should not lust after evil things, as they also lusted" (1 Corinthians 10:6). I believe Paul is saying, "All of these things – the wars, battles and conflicts – happened to Israel for our instruction. And scripture has recorded them to warn us about the spiritual battles we face. We learn important New Testament truths about Christ by studying the Old Testament aspects of Jehovah's nature."

So, what are these lessons we're to learn? What is the Holy Spirit saying to us in this battle between Israel and Amalek at Rephidim?

We learn from this battle that the Amalek spirit is still waging war against God's people.

The primary lesson to us here is that we're engaged in the same, ongoing spiritual battle. Paul writes, "We wrestle not against flesh and blood, but against principalities, against powers, against the rulers of the darkness of this world, against spiritual wickedness in high places" (Ephesians 6:12).

Amalek's first attacks on Israel were a type of guerrilla warfare in the wilderness. They blind-sided the Israelites at their points of weakness with quick, sneak attacks. For example, they sent soldiers to sneak up on Israel from behind while they were traveling. That way they could quietly kill off the old, weak and Infirm who couldn't keep up with the others.

Finally, Moses told Joshua, "Choose us out men, and go out, fight with Amalek" (Exodus 17:9). Joshua quickly put together a makeshift army of men with no battle experience whatsoever. These were shepherds and brick makers, not soldiers. They had no weapons, no shields, no chariots. Yet their enemy had all of these things, plus years of training. Certainly, the odds were against Israel.

Here is another lesson for us today: When the enemy comes against us like a flood, what does God tell his people to do? "Go in faith and fight – no matter what the odds." Our options during such times are clear: First, we can trust in God's Spirit to raise up a banner on our behalf. Or, second, we can surrender to unbelief, giving in to the enemy and becoming his slave.

I ask you, what do you usually do in such a moment? Do you sigh, give in to despair and say, "This battle is too big for me"? That's the reaction of many Christians today. They give up, thinking they just can't handle the conflict anymore. Yet our Lord clearly tells us, "I want you to fight the good fight of faith."

It's important for us to take a closer look at the men Joshua was leading into war. These men were not only inexperienced – they were the most messed-up bunch of soldiers you could find. Shortly before, these same men were ready to stone Moses because they'd run out of water. They accused him of bringing them out of Egypt to kill them and their families. Then they accused God of abandoning them, saying, "Is the Lord among us, or not?" (Exodus 17:7). Tell me, how can you go into battle for the Lord if you don't believe God is with you? This crew was made up of murmuring, unbelieving, miserable complainers. They constantly wavered between weak faith and stifling unbelief.

What a weak army God had to fight the devil. Keep in mind, the Lord had every right to destroy these ungrateful people or simply abandon them. Then he could raise up another, more faithful people. But God did nothing of the sort. Instead, he appointed these men as his army. And he told them, "Go and fight."

Today, we're no better than the Israelites were. We murmur and complain. We can see God perform one miracle after another for us, supplying our needs and blessing our lives. But when a crisis comes up, we panic, crying out, "Where's God? Why is he letting me go through this? I had it easier when I was a sinner." We may talk frequently about our growing faith, we may sing God's praises in church, we may raise our hands in glorious worship. But the moment the enemy comes against us, we crumble and cry, "Oh, Lord, this is too much for me."

What a marvelous picture of grace that God uses such weak, unworthy people to be soldiers in his army. And what a greater wonder of grace that he makes us more than conquerors against our enemy.

As Joshua led these wavering men into combat with the Amalekites, Moses, Aaron and Hur hiked up a hill overlooking the battlefield. Moses stood up in full view of the conflict below, holding up a wooden rod. "And it came to pass, when Moses held up his hand, that Israel prevailed: and when he let down his hand, Amalek prevailed" (Exodus 17:11).

What is this scene all about? What lesson does it signify to us about doing battle in God's army? Most commentaries suggest Moses' upraised hands represent intercession and prayer. In other words, as long as he raised his hands, he was interceding – and as long as he interceded, the battle went in Israel's favour. So, one clear lesson here is about our need for prayer and intercession in doing battle against Satan. Jesus himself spoke on this subject. When the disciples were unable to cast out a demon, Christ told them, "This kind goeth not out but by prayer and fasting" (Matthew 17:21).

Yet I see another meaning in this passage. And I believe it goes far beyond the subject of prayer and intercession by God's people. I suggest that the Lord wants to reveal the following to us:

This story is about Jesus – about the power and victory of his cross, and about the intercession he makes for us in glory.

Moses must have been fully aware that his actions were somehow representative of the coming messiah. He later prophesied, "The Lord thy God will raise up unto thee a Prophet from the midst of thee, of thy brethren, like unto me; unto him ye shall hearken" (Deuteronomy 18:15).

We see this demonstrated in the image of Moses carrying a wooden rod up the hill. This is another clear foreshadowing of Christ's journey up the hill of Golgotha. Moses' rod here represents the cross of Christ. Likewise, Moses' raising of his hands atop the hill represents the prayers and supplications of Christ our high priest.

As we envision Moses standing at the top of the hill, holding up the rod, we see yet another foreshadowing of Christ. This was a picture of Jesus on the cross at Calvary – looking down upon humanity and beholding the great conflict being waged against his body by Satan.

Moreover, whenever the Israelites looked up and saw Moses holding the rod, the battle turned in their favor. This points to Jesus' day, when Christ said, "I, if I be lifted up from the earth, will draw all men unto me" (John 12:32).

As the battle at Rephidim wore on, "Moses' hands were heavy" (Exodus 17:12). We see this same heaviness at Gethsemane, where Jesus' work of intercession grew heavy under the burden of man's sin. Matthew writes, "Then cometh Jesus ... and saith unto the disciples, Sit ye here, while I go and pray yonder ... and [he] began to be sorrowful and very heavy" (Matthew 26:36-37).

Yet another parallel to Christ occurs as Aaron and Hur try to aid Moses. "They took a stone, and put it under him, and he sat thereon" (Exodus 17:12). Evidently, from the moment Moses sat down, the battle swung completely toward the Israelites' favour. Now note what Hebrews says about Jesus: "When he had by himself purged our sins, sat down on the right hand of the Majesty on high" (Hebrews 1:3). "But this man, after he had offered one sacrifice for sins for ever, sat down on the right hand of God; from henceforth expecting till his enemies be made his footstool" (10: 12-13).

Finally, the rod that Moses held up provided the Israelites with a supernatural surge of power. And, ultimately, that power led them to victory over the Amalekites: "Joshua discomfited Amalek and his people with the edge of the sword" (Exodus 17:13). The Israelites' sudden strength must have totally confused the well-armed, well-trained Amalekites. Once again, we see an obvious parallel to the kind of supernatural power given to God's people in the New Testament. Paul writes, "The preaching of the cross is to them that perish foolishness; but unto us which are saved it is the power of God" (1 Corinthians 1:18).

Please don't misunderstand – I'm not saying that when Moses held up the rod, he thought, "This represents the cross our Lord will die on." Nor am I saying that when Moses sat down, he reasoned, "This foretells the time when the messiah will be seated at the right hand of God, in full authority." No, the battle Moses saw before him was real, with men fighting and dying, left and right. It was a very present conflict, having to do with flesh-and-blood Israelites. Yet, through this battle, God was trying to show his people that if they would trust his banner over them (represented by the upraised rod), he would lead them to victory.

Of course, at this point in history, Israel's victory over Amalek wasn't complete. Some of the Amalekites escaped to regroup and attack Israel again. But this entire passage evokes the image of Christ to come, when the victory over Satan would be complete.

Moses built an altar and called it Jehovah Nissi – Hebrew for "The Lord my banner, the Lord my ensign."

"Moses built an altar, and called the name of it Jehovah-nissi" (Exodus 17:15). Moses told Israel, "We've won the battle here today. And we can't forget that we were victorious because we serve Jehovah Nissi – the Lord, our banner. This victory had nothing to do with our strength or ability, or any great works we promised to do for God. We did nothing to earn the Lord's favour today. God himself is our banner – and our victory is totally the work of his hand."

I want to show you beyond any shadow of a doubt that Jehovah Nissi is also "the Lord Jesus, our banner." Isaiah saw this in the Pentateuch and in the prophets' writings. He stated, "In that day there shall be a root of Jesse, which shall stand for an ensign [banner] of the people; to it shall the Gentiles seek: and his rest shall be glorious" (Isaiah 11:10). "With the rod of his mouth, and with the breath of his lips shall he slay the wicked" (11:4). Of course, the root of Jesse whom Isaiah mentions is Jesus, who's also called "the son of David." Isaiah was declaring Christ to be the banner whom the world would rally under. Jesus alone would provide us with victory over Amalek and with sweet rest and peace.

In the Exodus passage we read at the beginning of this chapter, Moses clearly tied the revelation of Jehovah Nissi's name to every succeeding generation: "Moses built an altar, and called the name of it Jehovah-nissi: for he said, Because the Lord hath sworn that the Lord will have war with Amalek from generation to generation" (Exodus 17:15-16).

Two things are obvious from this passage: First, the revelation of Jehovah Nissi's name has to do with the spiritual warfare God declared against Amalek. And second, this warfare would continue from generation to generation.

Now the prophet Isaiah is declaring Jehovah Nissi – the Lord our banner – to a new generation. As he does, he clearly refers to the coming of Christ:

"There shall come forth a rod out of the stem of Jesse, and a Branch shall grow out of his roots: and the spirit of the Lord shall rest upon him, the spirit of wisdom and understanding, the spirit of counsel and might, the spirit of knowledge and of the fear of the Lord; and shall make him of quick understanding in the fear of the Lord: and he shall not judge after the sight of his eyes, neither reprove after the hearing of his ears: But with righteousness shall he judge the poor, and reprove with equity for the meek of the earth: and he shall smite the earth with the rod of his mouth, and with the breath of his lips shall he slay the wicked" (Isaiah 11:1-4).

From Abraham onward, all of God's righteous servants and prophets in the Old Testament had a revelation of Christ to come. In fact, Jehovah Nissi, the Lord our banner, is declared in both the Old and New Testaments. Abraham, Moses and Isaiah looked forward to his coming, saying, "This is the one who will be our banner." And Paul looked back to him, saying, "Everything in the Old Testament is about Jesus. Every battle, every conflict, every war we read about here gives us another revelation of who he is."

Jesus himself told his disciples, "Your forefathers longed to see all the things you see me doing. They saw me only in type. But you see me in reality." "Verily I say unto you, That many prophets and righteous men have desired to see those things which ye see, and have not seen them; and to hear those things which ye hear, and have not heard them" (Matthew 13:17).

Our forefathers didn't receive the promise. But they did embrace its future fulfillment by faith. Hebrews tells us, "These all died in faith, not having received the promises, but having seen them afar off, and were persuaded of them, and embraced them, and confessed that they were strangers and pilgrims on the earth" (Hebrews 11:13).

Let me show you what I believe Moses is saying to our generation.

In my opinion, Moses is telling the church of Jesus Christ today, "Jehovah Nissi delivered us from the demonic power of Amalek. And as long as the spirit of Amalek continues to rage against God's people, Jehovah Nissi will still be our banner. He will cover us through every future generation, down to the very end of time. Therefore, we are always to look to Jehovah Nissi. This is our secret to victory – the revelation of our Lord's nature toward us."

You may wonder: "Didn't Jesus end the battle with his victory on the cross? Wasn't his victory total and complete? After all, he was raised up by the Spirit's resurrection power, breaking the bonds of death. And when he ascended to heaven, he was beyond the devil's reach forever. The victory was, is, and forever will be Christ's. So, doesn't that mean the battle should be over?"

Yes, Jesus' victory on the cross was complete, total and absolute, as regarding the head. But we, his body, are still in a battle. You see, while Jesus sits victoriously as head in heaven at the right hand of the father, beyond Satan's reach, we remain his body here on earth. And the New Testament clearly states that we face a roaring lion who seeks to devour us. Therefore, we are still in a warfare. And we have to do battle daily with the principalities and powers of darkness – because the devil wars against the Christ in us. This is why Paul instructs us to take up our spiritual weapons by putting on the whole armour of God (see Ephesians 6). We are to fight the good fight of faith against the enemy, who's still alive and at work on earth. And the victory Jesus won will be ours as we resist the devil by faith.

I ask you: is Amalek attacking you right now? Are you experiencing some kind of spiritual warfare? Are you battling a temptation or lust? Is your enemy trying to seduce you into the love of pleasure more than the love of God? Are you plagued by a spirit of guilt, fear or condemnation? Is your marriage or family under attack? Are you sensing the enemy's tactics against you in your job or career? Has he come against you personally, bringing depression, weariness, or a strange, inexplicable restlessness?

It's vital for you to have a true biblical understanding of what's going on in your life right now.
You're in the midst of warfare, whether you want to
be or not. And once you adopt this biblical view of
warfare, your perspective on everything will
change.

First, you must understand that the devil is not
mad at you personally. Ultimately, his battle is not
with you. His hand is set against the throne of God.
Therefore, when Satan comes against you like a
flood, he's not just trying to get you to become a
fornicator or thief or alcoholic or pleasure-monger.
That isn't his goal or purpose in trying to seduce
your flesh. Rather, he does so for one reason:
because you are Christ's seed – and it's that holy
seed he's after.

Satan is still in a war against Christ. And since he
realizes he lost his battle against Jesus on earth, he
now tries to get to him through his seed. That's the
only way Satan expects to ever win against the
throne of God – by wiping out all of Christ's seed
from the earth. The devil believes if he can destroy
every Christian, he can still overcome. That's why
he seduces and tempts your flesh – because you've
come under the banner of Christ. So, yes, you are in
a battle, but it isn't your battle. It's a battle between
the devil and the throne of God.

Satan has one simple strategy against you in this
battle: he wants to convince you to give up on Jesus.
That's why he tries to terrify you, to cause you to
faint in your faith – so you'll distrust Christ and
desert him. He wants to make you run from the

battle, to leave the Lord's army and stop being his representative on earth. This is how the enemy plans to destroy the seed – by killing off Christ's army, one soldier at a time.

Tragically, many believers have already deserted Jesus. They say, "I tried, but the battle was too hard. I hoped, I prayed, I did everything I thought I should. And all along, I thought the Holy Spirit would be there for me. But in my hour of temptation, he was nowhere to be found. The battle was beyond me."

That is Satan's primary purpose in his battle against you: to totally discourage you. He wants to get you so focused on the awfulness of your sin, so persuaded you're powerless to resist temptation, so convinced God has left you alone, you'll no longer look up to Christ's victory on the cross.

This is why God gives us this word: "O Israel, ye approach this day unto battle against your enemies: let not your hearts faint, fear not, and do not tremble, neither be ye terrified because of them; for the Lord your God is he that goeth with you, to fight for you against your enemies, to save you" (Deuteronomy 20:3-4).

David knew the battle wasn't his. He knew it rested completely in God's hands. That's why this faithful man could stand without fear as he faced the giant Goliath. David said, "The battle isn't mine – it's the Lord's. You haven't defied me, Goliath – you've defied the living God. You've put your hand against his throne. And now you have to face him on the battlefield" (see 1 Samuel 17:47, 36).

Jehovah Nissi – Christ my banner – means he is the captain of my salvation.

Because of the revelation of the name Jehovah Nissi, we can declare the following:

"I'm kept by the rod upon the hill and the blood that was shed there. I'm also kept by my Lord's intercession for me at the right hand of the father. He has wiped out every one of my sins – annihilating them and removing them from my life completely. Moreover, I have the promise of his blood-sprinkling over every sin I will ever commit. All I have to do is come to the rod – to repent and look upon Christ and his victory on the cross. As long as I live, I have his complete forgiveness. And as long as I trust in the power of his blood, I'm empowered by the Holy Ghost. Jehovah Nissi is Christ my intercessor.

The prophet we see standing on the hill with his hands raised up is our risen Christ. And his banner over us is intercession. Right now, he stands before the very throne of God, pleading our case. Scripture says, "But this man, because he continueth ever, hath an unchangeable priesthood. Wherefore he is able also to save them to the uttermost that come unto God by him, seeing he ever liveth to make intercession for them" (Hebrew, 7:24-25).

Is your soul guilt-ridden, low, feeling condemned? Embrace the word of the Lord: "Who is he that condemneth? It is Christ that died, yea rather, that is risen again, who is even at the right hand of God, who also maketh intercession for us.

Who shall separate us from the love of Christ?"
(Romans 8:34-35).

The name Jehovah Nissi has meant two important
things in my life:

*1. The cross. This is something Jesus has already done
for me. In all my present battles, I'm able to look to his
victory on the cross. He has made provision to continually
sprinkle his blood on me, canceling out all my present
sins, whenever I repent and cry out to him.*

*2. Intercession. This is something Jesus does for me
now. My banner is seated at the right hand of the father,
acting as my high priest and intercessor. When he sat
down there, he did so to pray for me. And I trust fully in
the power and effectiveness of his prayers for me.*

It doesn't matter what your spiritual battle is – it
rests in the Lord's hands. And you are to place that
battle completely under his blood. Then remind
yourself, and the devil, that Jehovah Nissi is praying
for you. Jesus told us he prayed for his disciples, and
those prayers kept every one of his followers while
he was on earth. "I pray for them ... which thou hast
given me ... those that thou gavest me I have kept,
and none of them is lost, but the son of perdition"
(John 17:9, 12). If our Lord's prayers prevailed while
he was on earth, how much more will his prayers be
effective for us in glory? He has already assured us,
"None of my children will be lost."

Who can condemn you? What enemy can separate
you from the love of Christ? There is none. You are
victorious – because Jehovah Nissi is praying for
you.

Be careful, then, not to use the Lord's love and

grace to excuse sin. He is now praying for you to turn from all your iniquities and enter the reality of his power over the dominion of sin. He has promised to infuse you with the power of the Holy Ghost to live an overcoming life.

4

Jehovah Tsebaioth
"The Lord of Hosts"

"It came to pass, when Joshua was by Jericho, that he lifted up his eyes and looked, and, behold, there stood a man over against him with his sword drawn in his hand: and Joshua went unto him, and said unto him, Art thou for us, or for our adversaries? And he said, Nay; but as captain of the host of the Lord am I now come. And Joshua fell on his face to the earth, and did worship, and said unto him, What saith my lord unto his servant? And the captain of the Lord's host said unto Joshua, Loose thy shoe from off thy foot; for the place whereon thou standest is holy. And Joshua did so" (Joshua 5:13-15).

What a powerful revelation. In this scene, the Lord revealed himself to Joshua as Jehovah Tsebaioth – the Lord of hosts. As he stood before his humbled servant, he wielded a sword. And he commanded an army of angels, heavenly soldiers who stood ready to take up the fight for Israel.

God reveals himself as the Lord of hosts only to those who set their hearts and minds to walk before him in purity. He doesn't give this revelation to people who only want their sins forgiven and to make it to heaven someday. The luke-warm, the halfhearted and the fleshly believer will never know Jehovah Tsebaioth.

Tragically, a majority of Christians today aren't even aware of their need for Jehovah Tsebaioth. This is because they're not doing battle, not seeking victory, not moving forward in their walk with Christ. Instead, they've made peace with the sinful strongholds that grip them. Why would the Lord send his heavenly army to help such believers, when they're not even willing to take up the fight?

The Lord reserves his powerful revelation of a heavenly army only for those who declare war on their sin and unbelief. Such believers have decided they're going into the promised land, no matter what it costs them. And they're willing to do battle with anything that stands between them and the fullness of God's covenant promises.

Joshua was just such a believer. He was determined with all his heart, soul, mind and strength to go the distance with the Lord. This man was born in a generation of compromise, bitterness and rebellion. Yet Joshua stepped out from among his peers and drew a line in the sand. By his life he stated, "I refuse to be like this compromising crowd. I have a hunger in my heart for God. And I'm not going to allow this generation's filth and unbelief to corrupt me. I know I have yet to discover much about my Lord. He's made many covenant promises to his people, and I intend to lay hold of every one of those promises. So now, as I cross this line, I know there's no going back for me. I've set my heart to enter all

the way into God's promised rest. I'm determined to
resist, sacrifice, obey, surrender. I'll do anything
necessary to bring down all strongholds that stand
between me and total victory."

Joshua represents a holy remnant who are living
in this last hour. Like him, these lovers of Jesus are
determined to go all the way with the Lord. Their
hearts' sole cry is to walk in holiness, worthy of
Christ. Therefore, they yearn to be free of every false
thing, every stronghold of iniquity, every dominion
of besetting sins. They refuse to allow anything in
their lives that might drag them down from that
determination. They want nothing of the greed,
fame and pleasures of this world. And, like Joshua,
they have crossed a line. They've left behind the
world and its allurements, once and for all. And
they're passing over the Jordan to follow the Lord
into the fullness of his covenant promises.

Joshua was the leader of a new generation in
Israel. The previous generation ended up dying in
the wilderness because of their unbelief. Those
miserable people lived under a curse until every last
one of them died. But this hungry, new Joshua
Company began to seek God. They were ready to
declare war on anything that stood in their way of
entering into the fullness of the land God had promised them.

Just before Moses died, he received a supernatural vision of the Lord. In this vision, he saw God
"rid(ing) upon the heaven in thy help, and in his
excellency on the sky" (Deuteronomy 33:26). Moses
also saw God holding up his people, with his ever-

lasting arms supporting them underneath. The prophet declared that "the eternal God is thy refuge, and underneath are the everlasting arms" (33:27).

It was a wonderful revelation. Yet Joshua was given an even clearer picture of this image of the Lord. In the vision he received, Joshua saw this rider in the sky leading an army, a host of heavenly beings waiting to receive their next assignment.

I believe this revelation Joshua received of Jehovah Tsebaioth is meant for every devoted lover of Jesus today. Right now, hosts of heavenly beings are riding through the heavenlies on our behalf, waiting to receive their next assignment to fight for us. They're stationed all over the world, a troop here, a battalion there. They are the unseen forces of heaven, fighting against principalities and powers of darkness. I say to every lover of Jesus living today: we'd better believe we need God's heavenly hosts fighting on our behalf. We can't possibly combat hell's forces with any amount of human strength. Like the hungry, young believers in Joshua's day, the Joshua Company of this last hour can't move forward into God's promised victory without experiencing four things. These four things are required of everyone who would lay hold fully of God's covenant promises:

1. We have to cross over the Jordan.

"The priests that bare the ark of the covenant of the Lord stood firm on dry ground in the midst of the Jordan, and all the Israelites passed over on dry ground, until all the people were passed clean over Jordan" (Joshua 3:17).

The Jordan River has great significance in the life of every Christian. Like Israel, we come to our own Jordan crossing when we tire of the dead, dry Christianity we see all around us. We grow weary of the backslidden condition of the church – sick of the worldliness, unbelief and idolatry running rampant in denominations that long ago grieved away God's Spirit. We're totally disgusted with the wilderness experience we see represented in that old system. The Holy Spirit has stirred our hearts, and we realize we'll never be satisfied with the kind of life led by the carnal, pleasure-seeking masses.

Yet, as we turn inward to examine our own spiritual condition, we're sickened by what we see there also. Finally, we cry out, "Lord, I've had enough of this backslidden, ineffectual Christianity. I want to be delivered from the power of sin and materialism. And I want a heart that's pure and holy before you. I refuse to just drift along in these last days, satisfied with a lukewarm spirit. I want to be a light for Jesus amid this wicked generation. I'm determined to seek you, Lord, and to obtain your strength. I want to go all the way with you, no matter what the cost."

Have you set your heart to follow Jesus in this way? Have you followed the Joshua Company to the bank of the Jordan? If this is true of you, then you must face this fact: you've come to a place of death. When you cross the Jordan, you undergo a death to this world and everything in it.

Jesus is our example. As he was being baptized in

the Jordan, the heavenly father declared, "Behold my son, in whom I am well pleased. He's mine, and he represents me fully." The same happens with us when we undergo death to this world. As we come up on the other side, the Holy Spirit identifies us as God's own, declaring, "This is my beloved son, my beloved daughter." He's heard our cry for the Spirit to empower us to go all the way into his fullness. He's seen us seeking him for an overcoming life, free from all chains of sin, lust and pride. And he responds by marking us as entering into covenant with him.

Make no mistake about it, crossing the Jordan is a declaration of war. You're making a commitment that you're going to do battle with every besetting sin that stands in your way of obtaining God's fullness. You're crossing a line that says, "I won't live with this lust anymore. I'm walking toward Jesus, toward holiness and purity of heart. And I'm not looking back. I declare all-out war on this stronghold."

When Israel crossed the Jordan, they were going on the offensive. They knew as soon they got to the other side they would be in enemy territory. And when they arrived, word spread quickly among their enemies: "The Israelites are in the land, and they mean business. They're no longer wandering around aimlessly in the wilderness. Their God is once again doing wonders in their midst. And they're determined to take dominion."

Before Israel crossed over into the promised land, the enemy strongholds there remained unchal-

lenged for years. The Hittites, Canaanites and
Jebusites all had heard about Israel's wanderings in
the wilderness, and they weren't afraid of them. The
word about Israel was, "These people are harmless.
They've been talking about taking the offensive for
forty years now. But they're drifters, hopelessly
aimless. All we've seen them do is murmur and
complain. They're all talk. They don't live up to
what they say they believe about their God. They
don't even pray to him anymore. They must not
even believe he exists. We've got nothing to worry
about from these people."

Up to this time, the city of Jericho had its gates
open for trade. People came and went as they
pleased, unafraid of the Israelites' presence on the
wilderness side of the Jordan. But the moment Israel
crossed the river, everything changed. The inhabitants of Canaan sensed something serious going on
with God's people. The Israelites were suddenly in
the promised land. And Jericho promptly shut its
gates. The Bible says, "All the inhabitants of the land
faint because of you" (Joshua 2:9).

Just twenty-four hours before, these inhabitants
were laughing at the Israelites, saying they were a
joke. But within days, they saw the Israelites
marching fearlessly around the walls of their city.
The Canaanites trembled at the sight. Israel's presence there now was totally intimidating.

What an incredible turnaround in such a short
amount of time. Think about it: as Israel's soldiers
marched around the base of the city, they were easy
targets for the enemy's fiery arrows. Yet the men of

Jericho never tried to attack. Why? Apparently, they were so afraid that they couldn't even lift their arms to draw back their bows. Scripture says they simply had no courage left against God's people: "As soon as we had heard these things, our hearts did melt, neither did there remain any more courage in any man, because of you: for the Lord your God, he is God in heaven above, and in earth beneath" (Joshua 2:11).

What about your personal Jericho? For years now you've tried to coexist with your personal stronghold, wandering around aimlessly in a spiritual wilderness. The devil has mocked you, laughed at you, not taken your walk with Christ seriously. But now you've declared war – you've crossed your Jordan, and the enemy knows you're committed. James tells us, "Resist the devil, and he will flee from you" (James 4:7). When the enemy sees you coming at him, marching boldly on the offensive, he'll retreat in fear and shut the gates behind him, just as he did at Jericho.

Perhaps you've lived with a besetting sin for years: adultery, fornication, pornography, unbelief, doubt, stubbornness, rebellion, bitterness. Over time, the devil has used that one seduction to build up a stronghold in your soul. He has brought in principalities and powers of darkness to imbed walls around your heart. And year after year, those walls have grown thicker and stronger. Now there's simply no way you can humanly cast out such a stronghold. You need divine, unseen powers to work away on those walls for you. You need

Jehovah Tsebaioth to do the supernatural work of tearing them down.

That work begins the moment you stand up and declare war on your sin. You have to see your habit as a matter of life or death. And your Jordan is simply a determination you've made to get victory. By doing so, you become a warrior on the offensive. You declare you're no longer a wimp, that you're now unwilling to be a slave to Satan's devices and delusions. You renounce all ties to this filthy world. And you call on the Holy Ghost to empower you to wage war against all sin in your life. You declare, "I'm crossing a line, and I'm not going back. By the help of the Holy Spirit, I'm going to live a righteous, clean, holy life. It doesn't matter how wicked and vile the world around me becomes. I want to be part of God's Joshua Company." With this single resolve, you strike fear in the heart of Satan and all his hellish hosts.

This leads us to the second requirement of everyone who would go on to obtain God's promised victory:

2. We have to face the sharp knife of circumcision. I remember an old gospel song from my childhood called, "This Is Like Heaven to Me." The chorus goes, "Oh, this is like heaven to me, yes, this is like heaven to me. I have crossed over Jordan to Canaan's fair land, and this is like heaven to me." Whoever wrote that song never read Joshua 5. When the Israelites got to the other side of the Jordan, it was anything but heaven for them.

At first, Joshua's fresh young warriors probably thought they were in heaven. After all, they'd finally made it into the promised land. I imagine them falling on their faces and kissing the ground. Now they were ready for a fight, crying, "Let's go. We're going to tear down that walled city, brick by brick. We've got what it takes. And the Lord is on our side. Let us at 'em."

Yet, while these soldiers may have been pumping themselves up, Joshua sat by himself, quietly sharpening knives. He knew that enthusiasm and excitement alone weren't going to win any war. There would be a time to shout, but now wasn't the time. First these men had to face the knife of circumcision: "At that time the Lord said unto Joshua, Make thee sharp knives, and circumcise again the children of Israel the second time. And Joshua made him sharp knives, and circumcised the children of Israel at the hill of the foreskins" (Joshua 5:2-3).

Why would God require these men to be circumcised at this time? What was this scene all about?

Down through the centuries, an entire theology has been developed regarding the meaning of circumcision. Countless sermons have been preached on the subject, and many books have been written about it. Simply put, in both the Old and New Testaments, circumcision is an outward act that signifies something taking place in the heart. "Circumcise therefore the foreskin of your heart, and be no more stiffnecked" (Deuteronomy 10:16). "Circumcison is that of the heart, in the spirit, and not in the letter" (Romans 2:29). "In whom also ye are circumcised with the circumcision made without hands, in putting off the body of the sins of the flesh by the circumcision of Christ" (Colossians 2:11).

These soldiers' circumcision at Gilgal involved cutting flesh, but it also illustrated a spiritual occurrence. We know this from Moses' speech to Israel before he died. Moses foresaw the entire event of circumcision at Gilgal. He envisioned the gathering of God's people, ready to go to battle against Jericho. And he spoke prophetically to them about undergoing this significant rite: "The Lord thy God will bring thee into the land which thy fathers possessed, and thou shalt possess it; and he will do thee good, and multiply thee above thy fathers. And the Lord thy God will circumcise thine heart, and the heart of thy seed, to love the Lord thy God with all thine heart, and with all thy soul, that thou mayest live" (Deuteronomy 30:5-6).

The circumcision of Israel's soldiers here had to do with spiritual warfare. It signified the end of all confidence in the flesh. God knew these men's hearts were full of enthusiasm. He saw them chomping at the bit to tear down the satanic stronghold of Jericho. But the Lord commanded Joshua to put the knife to all of their posturing and self-confidence. They were to cut off all trust in their human strength to bring down the strongholds before them.

I can assure you, the next day these soldiers weren't shouting, dancing and singing, "This is like heaven to me." On the contrary, they were groaning in pain. God rendered them absolutely impotent. For a short season, they were helpless, utterly useless as soldiers. Scripture tells us, "They abode in their places in the camp, till they were whole" (Joshua 5:8).

What was God teaching his people here? He wanted them to see how completely powerless they were in the flesh. He wanted their impotence to sink deeply into their hearts, to convince them they could be saved only by faith in him. God intentionally brought them to this place of utter weakness, because he wanted to prove himself strong on their behalf.

If enemy scouts had spied on Israel at that moment, they would've seen the Israelites lying scattered about in absolute weakness. Once again, Israel's enemies could have attacked them and put an end to the entire warfare. Why didn't they? Why didn't the devil move in at that moment and destroy Israel in their weakened condition? I believe he wasn't allowed to, because heaven's unseen forces were at work protecting God's people. If the Lord had opened the Israelites' eyes, they would've seen fierce spiritual activity going on around them: fiery horses racing over the hills, angels influencing kings and leaders. These heavenly beings were battling down principalities and putting fear into people's hearts all across the land.

Through it all, God wanted to prove to Israel that he alone was their defense. He wanted to convince them, "This isn't your battle. Victory will never come through your own hands. It won't happen though your flesh, might or power. It will come to you only through my Spirit."

We can sing all the choruses we know about walking all over the devil. We can shout and rail against the enemy, shake our fists at him, try to bind him in Jesus' name. But it's all meaningless noise until we come under the knife of circumcision. All our skills, willpower and boasting are useless unless we cast our self-confidence onto the hill of foreskins.

Paul writes, "For we are the circumcision, which worship God in the spirit, and rejoice in Christ Jesus, and have no confidence in the flesh" (Philippians 3:3). The apostle then makes a powerful statement: "I have suffered the loss of all things, and do count them but dung, that I may win Christ" (3:8). What was Paul referring to here, when he said he gave up "all things" and cast them onto the hill of foreskins? He was talking about his great learning – his education, his human intellect, his own righteousness, his trust in his flesh. He said he counted all of these things to be nothing more than dung, worthy to be cast onto the ash heap. He was saying, "I've learned I absolutely have to do away with all confidence in the flesh. And that's a very painful lesson to learn."

Some time ago, I heard a minister on the radio preaching about persistence. He said, "If you really want to please the Lord, you just have to try harder." No – he's got it all wrong. You could spend your whole life trying harder, and yet you would fail at every turn. You could determine to do everything I've mentioned so far – draw a line, cross the Jordan, and leave behind all your lukewarmness and flirtation with the world – but you would still end up in defeat and despair. Determination is not enough.

New resolve is not enough. Getting fed up with your wilderness lifestyle is not enough. Your will – your human enthusiasm and fleshly flush of strength – has to be broken. You have to fully embrace the fact that you're powerless to bring down your personal Jericho. You need an army – an unseen, supernatural, heavenly force – to fight the evil powers that are dug into your stronghold.

Our ministry received a letter from a dear Christian housewife whose husband abandoned her, leaving her to raise six children alone. The couple had been married for twenty-five years, and this wife had spent all that time caring for their children and their household needs. Now, with her husband gone, she had no job skills, no means of income, and six needy children to feed. Her situation seemed hopeless. And she was absolutely panic-stricken.

This woman had nowhere to turn but to the Lord. She made up her mind she would trust God fully for all her needs. He would have to be her husband, her provider, her counsellor. So, first, she made sure she took all her children to church regularly. And when the cupboard was bare, she prayed in groceries. This continued for years – and all her needs were supplied, at every turn. She wrote, "There were times we had to kneel and ask God to send us our next meal. But in all those years, the Lord has always been faithful to provide for us. In fact, he's been better to my family than I ever could have imagined." Today, every one of that woman's children is serving the Lord. She just married off her oldest daughter to a wonderful man who's entering the ministry.

How did she get through it all? She did it by casting herself completely into the arms of her heavenly father. And she refused to put her confidence in man or in her own flesh. Try to imagine all the heavenly activity surrounding this family's comings and goings. I can just see the heavenly hosts moving here and there, giving divine directions to people all around her. They direct one Christian family to take her a bag of groceries. They instruct another to fill her car with gas. They tell her pastor to involve her family in church activities. God simply wouldn't allow the people in this woman's church community to sleep until they fulfilled what he prompted their hearts to do for her. The Lord had heavenly principalities working on her behalf everywhere. This is exactly how she made it, according to her testimony.

You'd be surprised at just how many angels God has commissioned to work for you right now. This is why he urges us, "Let me circumcise your heart. You can't accomplish anything through your intellect or abilities. You need me to perform this impossible work for you. So, turn to me. Trust me to do it. I have all the resources you need."

Only after the Israelites were circumcised were they ready to go to battle. They no longer had confidence in themselves or relied on their fleshly enthusiasm. As their bodies were being healed physically, their spirits were being calmed by God's Spirit. Now they were ready to listen to the Lord.

3. We have to experience the passover.

The Israelites had crossed the Jordan, declaring war on their stronghold. And they'd been circumcised, swearing off all confidence in their flesh. Now they had to experience the passover. "The children of Israel encamped in Gilgal, and kept the passover on the fourteenth day of the month at even in the plains of Jericho" (Joshua 5:10).

God instituted the passover celebration in Exodus 12 as a security measure for Israel. It was meant to protect them against destruction. First, a lamb was to be slain, and its blood was to be sprinkled over their doorposts. "And they shall take of the blood, and strike it on the two side posts and on the upper door post of the houses, where they shall eat it ... And the blood shall be to you for a token upon the houses where ye are: and when I see the blood, I will pass over you, and the plague shall not be upon you to destroy you, when I smite the land of Egypt" (Exodus 12:7, 13).

Passover was an annual observance. It was to be held during the month that Israel had come out of Egypt, and on the fourteenth day of that month. On that day, Israel's annual calendar began. It became known as the "beginning of months."

Amazingly, on the day the Israelites recovered from their circumcision at Gilgal, it was the fourteenth day of that first month. Moreover, they were in the forty-first year of having come out of Egypt. So, now, just as they were about to do battle against the stronghold in their promised land, the day came to celebrate the passover. (How perfect God's timing is. I believe this passage shows us the Lord has set a day and time for everything in our lives. It all takes place under his heavenly gaze and his divine control. I call this "Holy Ghost timing.")

That evening, the Israelites offered the passover sacrifice. They built an altar and brought forth an unblemished lamb to be slain. First, the animal's blood was drained into a vessel. Then a high priest dipped hyssop into the blood, and used it to sprinkle the blood over the people. Finally, the lamb's carcass was consumed by fire on the altar.

There, in the shadow of Jericho's great, high walls, God's people experienced the sprinkling of the blood of the lamb. This blood sprinkling signified that God saw his people released from the guilt of all their sins. "Without shedding of blood is no remission" (Hebrews 9:22).

I believe Joshua preached a powerful sermon at this passover service. What he actually said doesn't appear in scripture, but I think I know the nature of the sermon he delivered. He knew this new generation had ears to hear the voice of the Lord. They'd crossed the Jordan and declared war. And now they were ready to go all the way to obtain God's promises. But there was something remaining in their hearts that the Lord wanted to deal with.

Perhaps at this point Joshua reminded the people of what had happened just a short time earlier. Their hearts had been fully exposed. And now he recalled to them the last words Moses had spoken to them: "I know thy rebellion, and thy stiff neck: behold while I am yet alive with you this day, ye have been rebel-

lious against the Lord; and how much more after my
death?" (Deuteronomy 31:27). The original Hebrew
word for rebellious in this verse means bitter,
disobedient.

Joshua knew Moses was right: the people he was
leading now still had serious problems. They were
bent on backsliding, always falling back into unbelief. Moreover, as Joshua considered the people's
sins, he had to look at the condition of his own heart
as well. He knew he was as human as the other
Israelites. At times he'd been plagued with his own
doubts and questions.

Now Joshua stood before the crowd with a
dilemma. How could he remind the Israelites about
this exposure of their hearts, without making them
feel condemned? They were on the brink of going
into battle against the stronghold of Jericho. They
couldn't possibly make war against that fortified
enemy if they thought God was mad at them. If they
harboured thoughts of condemnation in the midst of
battle, they would become weak and lose heart.

Joshua knew he couldn't lead the people into
battle this way. I believe he told Israel the following,
in so many words: "Here we stand, a people chosen
and blessed by God. We're full of courage, ready to
lay down our lives to gain freedom and enter into
the fullness of God's promises. Yet our hearts have
been fully exposed. Many still carry roots of bitterness toward the Lord. And others have been disobedient to his word. How can we overcome the
stronghold of Jericho, unless our wicked hearts are
cleaned up? We can't just cast the rebellion and

bitterness out of ourselves. We don't have the power to do that."

This describes our dilemma today as well. None of us is without disobedience in some area. Our failure may be overt sin, or it may be evil thoughts that plague our minds. Both are reminiscent of our old life in the wilderness, before we were saved. And both hold us back from entering fully into God's victory.

There's only one hope for us: we must come to the blood. By the sprinkling of the blood of the lamb, our Lord will cover our sins and look upon us as purged from all iniquity. Thank God for the blood of the perfect lamb who was slain for us: "If the blood of bulls and of goats, and the ashes of an heifer sprinkling the unclean, sanctifieth to the purifying of the flesh: how much more shall the blood of Christ, who through the eternal Spirit offered himself without spot to God, purge your conscience from dead works to serve the living God?" (Hebrews 9:13-14).

After the Israelites observed the passover, they were secured by the blood of the lamb. They no longer had to carry the condemnation of their sin. The only thing that mattered now was how God viewed them. And he beheld them as pure: "He hath not beheld iniquity in Jacob, neither hath he seen perverseness in Israel: the Lord his God is with him, and the shout of a king is among them" (Numbers 23:21).

The Israelites could now enter into spiritual warfare knowing their king saw no iniquity in them.

Likewise, this is the only way we can go against our Jericho strongholds – by laying our sins on the lamb. If we don't, we're already defeated. The author of Hebrews tells us this is why God swore an oath to bless us by delivering us from all sin: "Wherein God ... confirmed it by an oath: that ... we might have a strong consolation ... which hope we have as an anchor of the soul" (Hebrews 6:17-19).

The Joshua Company was now over the Jordan – circumcised, secured by the blood, and anchored in God's forgiving grace. They were brimming with confidence in the Lord, able to move forward with no condemnation. This brought them to the fourth requirement:

4. We have to face the walled city of Jericho.
Every one of us has his own Jericho. I'm speaking of a walled-up stronghold that hinders us from moving forward into fullness in Christ. In almost every case, this stronghold is a single besetting sin – a habit, lust or character weakness that has become entrenched in us, surrounded by impregnable walls. Your Jericho may be pride, fear of man, an out-of-control temper, a roving eye, a root of bitterness. No matter what it is, you can be sure it's keeping you back from the marvelous things God has prepared for you.

You may be tempted to think, "I don't have any strongholds in my life. I'm not holding onto a beset-ting sin." Yet if you say you have no sin, you call God a liar. The apostle John writes, "If we say that we have no sin, we deceive ourselves, and the truth is not in us ... If we say that we have not sinned, we make him a liar, and his word is not in us" (1 John 1:8, 10). We all have our Jerichos. And we're terribly deceived if we sit around smugly congratulating ourselves, believing we don't have any strongholds we need to be delivered from.

Many Christians acknowledge their Jericho but refuse to declare war on it. Instead, they give up the battle, thinking, "This sin is too deep in me. Its roots are too strong, too entrenched. I can't do anything to break its hold on me. I'll just have to live with it and do the best I can. I'll have to keep asking Jesus for forgiveness, because there's nothing I can do to stop it."

But there are awful consequences to coexisting with your Jericho. We see this illustrated in Numbers 13-14, when the twelve Israelite spies came back from spying out the land. These men had just visited Jericho and were awed by the city's forbidding walls. Archaeologists suggest those walls were so wide that chariot races might have been held on top of them. Rahab had a house embedded in one of Jericho's famous walls, and many other homes were built into them as well. The mere sight of the city's high, thick walls was enough to send the Israelite spies back to their camp disheartened. Scripture says these men brought back an evil report to Israel: "The cities are walled, and very great ... We be not able to go up against the people; for they are stronger than we" (Numbers 13:28, 31).

When the other Israelites heard this news, they completely lost heart. They refused to go up against

Jericho and its walled fortress. What were the consequences of their refusal? The Lord told them: "Surely they shall not see the land which I sware unto their fathers, neither shall any of them that provoked me see it ... as ye have spoken in mine ears, so will I do to you: your carcasses shall fall in this wilderness ... in this wilderness they shall be consumed, and there they shall die. And the men, which Moses sent to search the land, who returned and made all the congregation to murmur against him, by bringing up a slander upon the land, even those men that did bring up the evil report upon the land, died by the plague before the Lord" (14:23, 28-29, 35-37).

This is what happens when you refuse to declare war on your besetting sin. If you try to coexist with your Jericho, you bring down a spiritual death on yourself. And your faith ends up on the ash heap.

My mind immediately turns to several examples. I remember a man here at Times Square Church who always carried a briefcase with him. After years of attending our church, the man took me aside one day and whispered that he wanted to show me what was inside. When he opened the briefcase, it was filled with piles of filthy pornography. He told me sadly, "I'm hopelessly addicted. I've tried for years to quit, but I can't. There's just no hope for me." Both his head and his heart had been fried by the habit he indulged. He was almost out of his mind from constantly entertaining thoughts of horrible lust. At some point he had resigned himself to it, deciding, "It's all too much for me to handle. This wall inside me is never going to come down."

A minister once wrote me this tragic confession: "Years ago, I grew bitter toward a pastor because of the abuse he heaped on me. I refused to deal with my bitterness. Instead, I told the Lord, 'Don't call me, I'll call you'. In other words, I said to God, 'If I ever get over this, I'll let you know. Just don't bother me about it now. I can't handle it'. It has now been over twenty years since I began harbouring the hurt this man caused me. And in all that time, God has never once spoken to me. I have to confess, the hurt I once harboured is still there." This minister, a man called to preach the gospel of grace, has been wandering in a wilderness for over two decades. His life is plagued by deadly bitterness.

As my mind goes back over the years, I see the faces of many once-great ministers of God – powerful, mightily used preachers – who refused to declare war on their sins. They never determined to do battle against their besetting habits: adulterous affairs, addictions to pornography, bitterness, anger, dishonest financial dealings, lust for fame. Instead, they allowed their Jericho to live on.

Finally, the Spirit of God left them. Many of these men divorced their wives and left the ministry. Some remarried younger women. In the process, they lost everything: their families, their ministries, their self-respect, the regard of their peers. Some settled for work at menial jobs. Yet, all the while, they should have been involved in God's work full-time, ministering the gospel in the calling they'd been given. Some became alcoholics who died on the streets. Others died of deadly diseases within a few years. I remember once seeing a fallen evangelist – a once-godly man I had admired as a boy – hobbling around with a cane. After a lifetime of adultery, his body had been emaciated by the disease of sin.

In every case, these men were robbed of a life of joy, peace, rest and God's favour. None of them entered into the fullness of God's promises. Instead, they were consumed in a wilderness of sin, their bodies left ravaged. It all happened because they refused to deal with the stronghold of a besetting sin.

God is telling everyone in his church today, in no uncertain terms: "Your Jericho has to come down."

As Joshua stood on a hill overlooking Jericho, he must have strategized for hours about how to bring down this formidable stronghold.

As Joshua contemplated the impregnable walls of Jericho, his mind must have been working overtime. "How is it possible to penetrate such an impossible stronghold when all you have at your disposal is an untrained army with a few swords? Do you dig under the walls? Do you try to scale them? Do you burn down the gates?"

God probably let his servant strategize until there simply was no strategy left. Eventually, Joshua must have realized there was no human way to get through those walls. It was an utterly hopeless situation. He had to resign himself to the fact it was going to take a miracle. He might have prayed, "God, unless you undertake this work, it can't be done."

Then, suddenly, a man appeared before Joshua, wielding a sword. Scripture describes the scene this way: *"It came to pass, when Joshua was by Jericho, that he lifted up his eyes and looked, and, behold, there stood a man over against him with his sword drawn in his hand: and Joshua went unto him, and said unto him, Art thou for us, or for our adversaries? And he said, Nay; but as captain of the host of the Lord am I now come. And Joshua fell on his face to the earth, and did worship, and said unto him, What saith my lord unto his servant? And the captain of the Lord's host said unto Joshua, Loose thy shoe from off thy foot; for the place whereon thou standest is holy. And Joshua did so"* (Joshua 5:13-15).

I believe with most Bible scholars that this captain of the Lord's host was Jesus. Joshua apparently recognized him as being Jehovah. Otherwise, he never would have bowed and worshipped him. He couldn't worship an angel.

Joshua cried out to this figure, "Are you for us, or against us?" At first glance, the captain's reply seems curt, aloof, even condescending. He avoids answering Joshua's question directly, replying instead, "I am the captain of the Lord's host." This phrase translates in Hebrew as, "I am come as Jehovah Tsebaioth." He's saying, in other words, "You've asked the wrong question, Joshua. There's no side for me to be on. This war isn't between you and Jericho. It's a war between Jehovah and Satan. And I'm Jehovah Tsebaioth, captain of the Lord's heavenly army. You need to know this is not your battle, but mine."

Here is the key to all victory. You've crossed the Jordan, you've been circumcised, you've been blood secured – yet you still face an overwhelming battle. This warfare is totally beyond your strength and ability. So the Lord comes to you with a powerful assurance: "You have to see that this battle is not yours, but mine. I'm committed to do all the fighting for you."

Joshua immediately understood this revelation of God's power and might. He must have been totally relieved to hand over his sword. He probably said, "Thank you, Lord. I didn't have a plan." I imagine Jesus answering, "Of course you didn't. There is no plan for man in this kind of warfare. The battle is all mine."

The devil had infiltrated Jericho years before the Israelites arrived, making sure it was fortified by his own unseen powers. He'd been fully aware of God's promise to give the land to Israel. So he directed his demonic forces to dig into the city with every conceivable armament. It was a massive effort from hell to thwart the seed, to keep it from moving forward to its fulfillment in the coming messiah.

So it is with your besetting sin. Your Jericho has become entrenched in you by the devil's unseen forces. This doesn't mean you're demon possessed. It simply means there's one stronghold left, one hidden place in your flesh where the devil has dug in and refused to let go. You can't enter into the Lord's fullness until that stronghold comes down. It simply has to be dealt with. Yet you have no power to do battle against it.

Only the Lord's unseen army can conquer this stronghold. On your own, you could strategize for years without ever coming up with an effective plan. You'd end up thinking, "There's no way I can ever defeat this enemy. Time after time, battle after battle, it has proven too strong for me. I know I'll only fall again if I keep trying to go up against it. I don't even have the strength to try anymore. I guess I'll always be at the mercy and power of this enemy."

No, never! The Lord is telling you, "I'm going to fight this battle for you. I have the power to dig out those demon powers. You've already done all you need to do. You've crossed your Jordan, you've been circumcised, and you've been blood secured. Now you only need to move forward at my word. Soon you'll see me bring down this stronghold before your eyes."

This is just what Christ was communicating to Joshua when he appeared to him. He was saying, "Joshua, the enemy has fortified Jericho with unseen principalities and powers of darkness. It's going to take an unseen host from glory to cast him down. So, I come to you now as Jehovah Tsebaioth – captain of the Lord of hosts. I have at my command a huge, mighty army, with troops, chariots and horses you know nothing about. This is not your battle – it's the Lord's. And the host of heavenly beings who act on my command are going to tear these walls down. They're going to wipe out Jericho from the face of the earth forever. Your job in this battle is just to keep moving on. Simply walk in obedience to my word. My unseen host will deal with bringing down this stronghold."

Many Christians today become overwhelmed as they try to confront their strongholds. When they see their Jericho towering before them, they panic. And as they contemplate doing battle against this enemy, they begin to wither. Soon, the enemy has beaten them back into the wilderness. He's convinced them they have to remain helpless until they die. But Jehovah Tsebaioth appears to them with these words of reassurance: "You don't have to fear this enemy. Just come under the blood. I'll cover you with all manner of divine protection. Keep walking and talking with me. All the while, I'll be doing battle for you. I have a whole host at my disposal to do war against your Jericho. You have to know that the forces of Jehovah Tsebaioth are always at work on your behalf."

As Israel kept moving forward toward Jericho, a whirl-wind of activity took place silently in the unseen world. Princes of glory did combat with the principalities of hell. And each day, as the Israelites marched around Jericho, heavenly forces were at work undermining the city's walls. God's hosts loosened every brick and weakened the foundations.

What do you think the Israelites thought as they marched daily around Jericho's walls? I believe they probably had doubts about the battle. After all, during the whole week they marched, they never saw any evidence that God was at work. They simply did their marching every day and went back to camp at night. Not once during that week did they see any visible results of a heavenly host's work on their behalf.

Then the seventh day came. In obedience to God's command, the Israelites blew their trumpets – and Jericho's mighty walls came tumbling down. We can't possibly imagine the thunderous sound made by that great crash, as the enemy's centuries-old stronghold was brought to nothing. Yet, It wasn't the Israelites' shouting that brought down those walls. It was the hosts of Jehovah pushing them down with supernatural might.

What about the enemy's stronghold in your life? Have you lived for years with a besetting sin you despise, never gaining victory over it? As you face it now, are you at a loss about what to do? I tell you, it's time to declare war on your Jericho. Give up all hope of ever overcoming it by your own strength and willpower. Instead, bow down to the power of the Holy Ghost. Hand your sword over to God. And trust in his covenant promise to defeat all your enemies. You'll discover Jehovah Tsebaioth, the Lord of hosts. And you'll see him go to work for you.

Your role is simply to keep moving forward in faith and obedience. Don't faint or allow yourself to despair. Just be faithful to keep walking on with Jesus. He's the captain of the Lord's hosts, and he's faithful to take down your stronghold. He gave Israel specific directions for battle, and he'll give you directions for your path as well. You can trust him to direct his hosts of angels to do his bidding on your behalf.

Of course, we can get discouraged in our battle against Jericho if we don't see results right away. We may think, "I'm moving forward in obedience, just as the Lord directed me. I'm trusting him with all my heart. And I'm not fearful anymore. But this stronghold is still in me. I don't see it budging at all. Is the Lord working for me, or not? Where are the results?"

You have to remember Israel's example at Jericho. Those lovers of God couldn't see the battle going on in the heavenlies. But in the unseen world, God's army was winning victory after victory. And on the seventh day, that great host cried, "Let us finish the work." They pushed down the walls, crushing all of Jericho's inner structures. And they put every evil defender to flight.

Likewise, you may not see immediate results. Yet, while you're walking with Jesus – moving forward in faith, fully persuaded you're secured by the blood – your Lord's hosts are waging war for you. They're doing battle against the demonic principality that has entrenched itself in your stronghold. And you can rest assured, your Jericho is coming down. Jehovah Tsebaioth, the Lord of hosts, is at work for you. So, just keep walking, keep moving on. Your day of total victory is soon to come.

5

Jehovah Shalom
"The Lord our Peace"

Knowing and believing in God's character as revealed in his names provides great protection against enemy attack. God declared through Hosea, "My people are destroyed for lack of knowledge" (Hosea 4:6). The implication here is powerful. God is telling us that having an intimate knowledge of his nature and character, as revealed through his names, is a powerful shield against Satan's lies.

This brings us to another of our Lord's names: Jehovah Shalom. We find this name mentioned in the book of Judges. Here, the Lord revealed himself to Gideon in the form of an angel: "When Gideon perceived that he was an angel of the Lord, Gideon said, Alas, O Lord God! For because I have seen an angel of the Lord face to face. And the Lord said unto him, Peace be unto thee; fear not: thou shalt not die. Then Gideon built an altar there unto the Lord, and called it Jehovah Shalom" (Judges 6:22-24).

What does this name, Jehovah Shalom, mean exactly? I could digress here into a discussion of the many meanings of this well-known Hebrew word shalom. Suffice it to say, shalom is one of the most meaningful expressions in the Hebrew language. To this day, the word is held dear in the hearts of most Jews. Even as a Christian, you've probably heard the warm greeting, "Shalom", being used. Perhaps you've used it on occasion, lifting your hand in greeting to your brothers and sisters in Christ, saying, "Shalom! The peace of God be with you." Somehow, you've learned that this Jewish expression has something to do with having peace.

As a noun, the Hebrew word shalom means completeness, health, welfare. It implies being whole, in harmony with God and man, having wholesome relationships. It also indicates a state of being at ease – not restless, having peace both inwardly and outwardly, being at rest both spiritually and emotionally. In short, shalom signifies wholeness in a life or work. And as a verb, shalom means to be completed or finished, or to make peace.

I've read several scholarly works concerning these wonderfully redemptive definitions of shalom. In my studies, I've discovered that the word's multiple meanings are wonderfully varied and deep. This is especially true of shalom as it relates to Jesus Christ, the prince of peace, who provides his people with supernatural peace in every dimension of life.

Yet, once more, I'm driven to ask, "What does this particular name of God have to do with me and with the church today? What is the Lord trying to say to his people through this name, Jehovah Shalom?"

I must keep reminding you, every time God revealed a characteristic of his nature to someone, that person was in a time of crisis. The revelation always came when God's servant needed a fresh vision of the Lord to see him through. And each time, God brought forth a specific aspect of his nature to instill in his servant the faith needed to accomplish his eternal purpose.

The revelation of Jehovah Shalom was given to one such man in crisis – Gideon. As we explore this passage in full, we'll see that the only way Gideon could have received such a revelation was through the Holy Ghost. And it changed Gideon's life and future.

In his great mercy, the Lord sent a warning to Israel. Out of nowhere, an angel appeared to God's people at Bochim, delivering an awesome rebuke. "An angel of the Lord came up from Gilgal to Bochim, and said, I made you to go up out of Egypt, and have brought you unto the land which I sware unto your fathers; and I said, I will never break my covenant with you. And ye shall make no league with the inhabitants of this land; ye shall throw down their altars: but ye have not obeyed my voice: why have ye done this? Wherefore I also said, I will not drive them out from before you; but they shall be as thorns in your sides, and their gods shall be a snare unto you" (Judges 2:1-3).

This was a stern warning to a compromised nation. Yet I believe it was also meant for every generation to come, including the church today, upon whom the ends of the world have come. The Lord is giving us the same kind of warning:

"I brought you up out of the bondage of sin. I

delivered you and set you free from everything that bound you. Then, in my love for you, I brought you into a place of mercy and blessing. What did I ask of you in return? I commanded you to separate yourselves from the things of this world. I told you to flee its evil – to avoid getting entangled in its pleasures, to forsake everything having to do with its idolatry. Nothing of flesh or sin could remain in your life. You were to rid yourselves completely of everything that would rob you of power to stand before your enemy.

"Then I gave you a promise. I said if you would obey me on this one matter – if you refused to spare a single wicked way, desiring a pure heart – I would supply you with all the power you needed to remain free. I would send my Spirit to empower you. And through his strength, you would be able to utterly mortify every hindrance in your life. Nothing could keep you from being brought into my fullness.

"For years now, I've lovingly warned you to forsake your lusts. I've laid out my word clearly before you, in gentleness and kindness. I've sent messenger after messenger to remind you that you can't coexist with your sin or allow any compromise. Yet you persist in clinging to your idols. Why do you continue to disobey me? How can you not see the danger you're in? How can you keep coddling your idol, when it has served only to deepen your greed, lust and materialism? You thought you could contain your lusts, keep them on a leash. But now they've led you straight into the enemy's hands."

When the Israelites heard this reproving word, they were convicted to the point of tears. The Bible tells us, "It came to pass, when the angel of the Lord spake these words unto all the children of Israel, that the people lifted up their voice, and wept. And they called the name of that place Bochim" (Judges 2:4-5). The name Bochim means "a place of weeping and wailing."

I believe the Israelites' tears were real. The people felt awful about their sin, and they expressed their anguish openly. Yet, sadly, their conviction was short-lived. Scripture says they still didn't let go of their idols. They may have been good weepers, but none of them brought his idols to the altar to be destroyed. They thought they could go forth in service to the Lord while clutching their filthy idols.

Here's another important lesson for us today: In itself, exposure of sin cannot deliver anyone from bondage. Let's say your sin is exposed publicly. It brings you sadness, sorrow and humiliation. It may even cause you to weep mightily. Yet this doesn't mean you've been healed of your sin. The truth is, weeping and wailing often accompany a shallow, halfhearted repentance. The real fruit of genuine repentance isn't just tears of grief, but a willingness to forsake the sin that led to such sorrow.

I've personally witnessed the so-called open confessions of many ministers and church leaders who were caught in sin. When their lusts were exposed – bondages such as adultery, alcoholism, pornography – these men were overcome with emotion. They cried out publicly, "Yes, I've sinned."

Great tears poured down their cheeks, and they voiced pitiful cries of anguish.

Suddenly, the people surrounding these men set aside their shock, hurt and anger. They were moved to compassion for their minister. So they gathered around him, offering comfort, support and pledges of restoration. That is the Christ-like thing to do.

Yet, within a short period of time, the supposedly repentant minister went straight back to his sin. His repentance was shallow, halfhearted and ultimately self-serving. This has taught me an important lesson over the years: it's not enough merely to weep over your sins.

That's the exact message Malachi gave to a nation of adulterous Israelite men. The prophet cried out, "This have ye done again, covering the altar of the Lord with tears, with weeping, and with crying out, insomuch that he [God] regardeth not the offering" (Malachi 2:13). Malachi was saying, in essence, "You come to the altar weeping big tears, ready to offer a great sacrifice. But God sees the way you're still deceiving your wife. On the outside, you're repentant, grieving, sorrowful. But inside, you continue your treachery. You refuse to let go of your soulish and adulterous relationship."

The book of Judges is one of the saddest, most tragic chapters in the history of God's people. Consider the final, summary verse of this Old Testament book: "In those days there was no king in Israel: every man did that which was right in his own eyes" (Judges 21:25). That's where it all ended – with each of God's people doing what he thought was right for himself. Everyone was able to give an excuse for his own sin and evil behaviour. And few were deeply convicted by God's word.

Yet the entire book of Judges is more than the tragic history of the backsliding of Israel. It's also the story of our times, reflecting a church filled with believers who refuse to forsake their secret sin.

I see something taking place in the church all over the world today that grieves God's heart: a widespread apathy toward sin.

God's people today are no longer outraged about the filth and evil bombarding their lives and homes. On the contrary, millions of believers sit by passively and let their minds become saturated with sensual movies, videos, television, the Internet, magazines and other media. Unbelievably, these Christians willingly allow their lusts to be fed as their imaginations are filled with deep roots of evil.

If you think I'm focusing too much on the secret sins of Christians, then I say you're out of touch with what's happening in the world today. You know nothing of how widespread the infection of sin is among God's people. I cite to you, for example, the scores of Christians who flock to movie theaters each week and hear the name of Christ continually used as a curse word. I've never understood how anyone who fears almighty God and wishes to walk righteously before him can sit by idly as the Lord's name is being damned. That's simply beyond my comprehension. Yet multitudes of believers are doing just that. Little by little, they're drifting deeper into pits of secret, hidden sin. And, slowly but surely, their sense of conviction is being drained out of them. They don't realize it, but their minds are being corrupted by what they're allowing their eyes to feast on.

Yet, in his great mercy, God is always faithful to send prophets to warn his people. And today the Lord is sending us his holy watchmen – preachers, teachers, evangelists – with warnings to heed his word: "You must utterly destroy your besetting sin. You simply can't allow any evil way to remain in you. You have to declare war on the lusts and seductions of this age."

The Bible warns that if we continue to hold onto our secret sins, we'll eventually forsake God and be given over to our lusts. Our Lord may deal with us patiently, month after month, year after year. He may send us compassionate warnings through his faithful watchmen. But ultimately, if we refuse to heed his word, we'll slowly drift away from him completely. And we'll finally become a helpless prey before our enemy.

This is just what happened to Israel. The Bible tells us, "They forsook the Lord God of their fathers ... and followed other gods ... and provoked the Lord to anger ... and he delivered them into the hands of spoilers that spoiled them, and he sold them into the hands of their enemies round about, so that they could not any longer stand before their enemies ... the hand of the Lord was against them for evil ... and they were greatly distressed" (Judges 2:12-15).

Time after time, it was the same old story. Israel always promised to obey, but their words had no substance. They were never able to totally overcome their enemies or enjoy a lasting victory. Try to imagine the scores of Israelites who were lost during those long periods of sin and backsliding. If they had only embraced God's word when they heard it, they would've had the strength to withstand the hostile attacks of their enemies. But instead, they never allowed the preaching and teaching they heard to go any deeper than the surface. They never allowed the true fear of God to take root in their hearts. And they ended up being an easy prey for their enemies.

For seven years Israel paid a terrible price for their sins.

Judges 6 describes an awful scenario in Israel:
"The children of Israel did evil in the sight of the Lord: and the Lord delivered them into the hand of Midian seven years. And the hand of Midian prevailed against Israel: and because of the Midianites the children of Israel made them the dens which are in the mountains, and caves, and strong-holds. And so it was, when Israel had sown, that the Midianites came up, and the Amalekites, and the children of the east, even they came up against them; and they encamped against them, and destroyed the increase of the earth ... and left no sustenance for Israel, neither sheep, nor ox, nor ass.

"For they came up with their cattle and their tents,

and they came as grasshoppers for multitude; for both they and their camels were without number: and they entered into the land to destroy it. And Israel was greatly impoverished because of the Midianites; and the children of Israel cried unto the Lord" (Judges 6: 1-6).

Every year at harvest time, Israel was invaded by the Midianites. These enemies knew exactly when Israel's fields and vineyards became ripe and when the cattle gave birth. And for seven straight years, they migrated to Israel's borders on their camels, camped just beyond the outskirts, and waited. Then, when the time was right, they swooped down on Israel like locusts. They descended on the fields, taking everything in sight – fruit, crops, cattle. They literally wiped out the harvest, leaving God's people impoverished: "They ... destroyed the increase of the earth ... and left no sustenance for Israel" (6:4).

The Israelites couldn't understand why they were so harassed year after year. How could God allow their enemies to plunder them? After all, they had enjoyed forty years of prosperity under the prophetess Deborah. Why couldn't they stand up to the Midianites now and thwart these enemies' attacks? What had brought Israel to such a shameful level of cowardice? Wasn't God on their side, working on their behalf? If he was, why did they have to live in continual fear and poverty?

The Israelites were dumbfounded by it all. For years they had to live in caves for protection. They held prayer meetings in those caves, crying out to God, "Lord, we haven't forsaken you. You see us

calling on you day after day, weeping and interceding. Please, tell us, why is this happening? Why
do we have to endure so much trouble from our
enemies? Why don't we enjoy your peace anymore,
as we did under your servant Deborah? Why don't
we see you working on our behalf?"

Let me point out here that not all trouble which
comes upon believers is a result of sin. The Psalmist
writes, "Many are the afflictions of the righteous"
(Psalm 34:19). Yet note the second half of this verse:
"But the Lord delivereth him out of them all."
According to God's word, our Lord, in his time,
delivers his righteous servants out of their afflictions. They don't have to live in a constant state of
distress. They enjoy peace in their times of trial.
They may undergo seasons of affliction, but the
Lord is forever present to reassure them and deliver
them. Eventually, night turns to day.

This wasn't the case with Israel in Judges 6. Why
did the people have to endure constant distress? It
was because of their continual idolatry. They acted
holy before God, offering up prayers of weeping
and intercession. But as soon as their prayer meetings ended, they sneaked off to kneel before their
altars of Baal. In fact, throughout those seven years
of raids from the Midianites, Gideon's father, Joash,
kept an altar to Baal in his backyard. Why would
any Israelite do such a thing? He did so because, like
the other Israelites, he was jealous of the prosperity
the Midianites enjoyed. The Israelites thought, "Our
enemies are prospering. They've got our fruit and
provisions. Their god provides them with every-

thing while we sit here starving. Those Midianites must have one powerful god. Obviously, we can't afford to offend him." So the Lord's people became hyprocrites, two-faced worshipers. They gave lip service to Jehovah while paying tribute to another god.

At the very height of Israel's poverty, God sent another prophet to expose his people's sin. He wanted to show them exactly why they were distressed and impoverished. Scripture describes the scene this way:

"It came to pass, when the children of Israel cried unto the Lord because of the Midianites, that the Lord sent a prophet unto the children of Israel, which said unto them, Thus saith the Lord God of Israel, I brought you up from Egypt, and brought you forth out of the house of bondage; and I delivered you out of the hand of the Egyptians, and out of the hand of all that oppressed you, and drove them out from before you, and gave you their land; and I said unto you, I am the Lord your God; fear not the gods of the Amorites, in whose land ye dwell: but ye have not obeyed my voice" (Judges 6:7-10).

Who was the unnamed prophet who delivered this word? Scripture makes it clear, this stranger was the Lord himself (a Christophany). Often in the Old Testament, Christ is called "the angel of the Lord." Later in this same passage, we see the stranger referred to that way: "There came an angel of the Lord ... and the angel of the Lord appeared to him [Gideon]" (6:11-12). Then, just a few verses down, we see this angelic figure referred to as the Lord: "The Lord said unto him [Gideon], Peace be unto thee; fear not" (6:23).

When the unnamed prophet appeared on the scene, Gideon and his family were among the poorest of Israel's poor. They were living off the handfuls of grain Gideon brought home from a hidden threshing floor. Gideon was trying to eke out a living by scavenging any leftover wheat he could find. Now, as the angel of the Lord appeared, he said to Gideon: "The Lord is with thee, thou mighty man of valour" (6:12).

On the surface, these words may seem puzzling. God was speaking to a man who, like every other Israelite, had sat by and done nothing for seven years. Indeed, in all the years the Midianites attacked Israel, Gideon hadn't displayed a single evidence of valour. He hadn't even protested against his father's pagan altar. Like everyone else, Gideon had lived in fear and bondage.

Yet now the Lord was instructing this man, "Go in this thy might, and thou shalt save Israel from the hand of the Midianites: have not I sent thee?" (6:14). What might was the Lord talking about here? Where in this story do we read of any infusion of strength or power into Gideon? Did something supernatural happen during this exchange, so that Gideon's doubt and fear were transformed into might? Or, was he supposed to claim some divine vigor by faith?

Clearly, something happened to Gideon in this scene. Scripture indicates there was a definite transfer of power into him, an infusion of might from the Holy Ghost. We find a clue to this divine infusion in verse 14, which begins, "The Lord looked upon him ..." The Hebrew verb for looked in this verse is the same verb used in Genesis 32:30, when Jacob wrestled with the Lord. That verse reads, "Jacob called the name of the place Peniel: for I have seen God face to face, and my life is preserved." Jacob was saying, in essence, "God looked me right in the face."

What was the outcome of Jacob's face-to-face encounter with the Lord? Scripture tells us, "As a prince hast thou power with God and with men, and hast prevailed" (Genesis 32:28). Evidently, a transfer of power took place when Jesus looked Jacob in the eye. With this single gesture from the Lord, Jacob received an infusion of supernatural strength that prepared him to face any foe. The apostle Paul describes this kind of supernatural transfer in New Testament terms: "We all, with open face beholding as in a glass the glory of the Lord, are changed into the same image from glory to glory" (2 Corinthians 3:18).

Judges is telling us that Gideon had direct communion with God through this kind of face-to-face encounter. You might ask, "How could this be? Doesn't the Bible say it's impossible for any human being to see God and live?" You're absolutely right. The apostle John writes, "No man hath seen God at any time" (1 John 4:12). And Paul concurs, writing, "The blessed and only Potentate, the King of kings, and Lord of lords; who only hath immortality, dwelling in the light which no man can approach unto; whom no man hath seen, nor can see" (1 Timothy 6:15-16).

Yet John qualifies his statement with this verse: "No man hath seen God at any time; [but] the only begotten Son, which is in the bosom of the Father, he hath declared him" (John 1:18). John is saying, in other words, "Jesus has manifested the Father to us. We see the essence of the Father when we look at Christ, the son." John writes elsewhere, "The Word was made flesh, and dwelt among us, (and we beheld his glory, the glory as of the only begotten of the Father,) full of grace and truth" (John 1:14). John adds that long before Jesus' birth, Christ "was in the world, and the world was made by him, and the world knew him not" (1: 10).

Scripture makes it clear: over the centuries, people stood face to face with the mediator, Christ, and were changed by the experience. From Jacob at Peniel, to Moses on the mount, to Daniel, and down to this very day, men and women have been infused with Holy Ghost power just by beholding the Lord's countenance. And here in Judges, as Gideon communed with the Lord face to face, he also was being infused with a transforming power. It was a power that would provide Israel with deliverance.

"For they [Israel] got not the land in possession by their own sword, neither did their own arm save them: but by thy right hand, and thine arm, and the light of thy countenance, because thou hadst a favour unto them" (Psalm 44:3). Israel hadn't obtained the promised land through any innate power, authority or ability of their own. They'd received everything through their face-to-face encounters with the Lord. Every blessing had come to them not by power, nor by might, but by the glory of God's countenance.

The power and might Gideon received from the Lord couldn't be released in him until he knew with whom he was dealing.

This supernatural transfer of power totally transformed Gideon. In the blink of an eye, he turned from a coward into a mighty warrior. Yet, amazingly, Gideon still had no idea he was dealing with the Lord. This passage implies that he treated Christ as casually as he would treat any other human being. In fact, Gideon asked the stranger to give him a sign to prove he was from the Lord. He demanded, "If now I have found grace in thy sight, then shew me a sign that thou talkest with me" (Judges 6:17). Can you imagine such audacity? It's as if Gideon were saying to Jesus, "If you've truly been sent from God, then do something that convinces me you're actually who you say you are."

Gideon also tried to strike a sort of deal with the Lord. He said to him, "I'd like you to sit down and share a meal with me. So, I'm going into the kitchen now to prepare the food. Please, do me a favour and wait here until I bring it out" (see Judges 6:17-18). What Gideon did here is unfathomable to me. He actually put God on hold! Yet the Lord responded with grace, saying, "I will tarry until thou come again" (6:18).

After a while, Gideon returned with the food – a lamb, unleavened bread and broth. Yet, before he could set the meal on the table, the Lord instructed him to place the food on a nearby stone. Then he directed Gideon to pour the broth over it all. Gideon did as he was told, and the Lord promptly lifted his staff and touched the food with it. Suddenly, fire shot out of the rock and consumed the entire meal. Then, in an instant, the Lord disappeared as quickly as he had come. (He might even have vanished in the flame, as he later did before Samson's father, Manoah: "It came to pass, when the flame went up toward heaven from off the altar, that the angel of the Lord ascended in the flame of the altar" [Judges 13:20].)

Gideon was flabbergasted. The Bible says, "When Gideon perceived that he was an angel of the Lord, Gideon said, Alas, O Lord God! For because I have seen an angel of the Lord face to face" (622). Why was Gideon so shaken? He realized what God's word said: "There shall no man see me, and live" (Exodus 33:20). Suddenly, the truth exploded in Gideon's soul. He realized, "Oh, no – this was God almighty I just encountered. And I dealt with him casually the whole time. I treated him as if he were a mortal, just like me."

Gideon knew this was serious business. That's why he exclaimed, "Alas, O Lord God." The word alas here is an exclamation of sorrow, regret and grief, with an apprehension of danger. Think of what must have gone through Gideon's mind: "I've been toying with the creator of the universe. I didn't respond to him as holy, almighty God. Instead, I tested him, putting him on trial, accusing him of forsaking his chosen people. I even had the gall to ask him for a sign to prove he wasn't a fake. Woe is me – I'm as good as dead!"

We see this same kind of casual attitude toward almighty God in many churches today. Too often Christians conceive of the Lord as someone just like themselves: a buddy, a friend, someone to go have a good time with. Don't mistake my meaning here; I don't mind when godly people use endearing terms such as Daddy to describe the Lord. But too many believers have made God out to be a sugar daddy, a doting figure. They conceive of him as someone who merely lectures them when they sin, suggesting, "Try to do better next time."

This image of God is one reason why there's such widespread permissiveness in the church today. Casual Christians have no vision of a holy God. So they have no motivation to utterly destroy their besetting habit. Instead, they end up coexisting with their sin, coddling their lusts. This travesty in the church leads directly to the kind of tragic end Judges describes: everyone does what's right in his own eyes.

When the Lord's true identity became clear to Gideon, this man's eyes were opened to truth. He remembered the message of the unnamed prophet. And suddenly, he was filled with the righteous fear of God. Gideon thought, "It's true – our own sin and disobedience have brought down all this distress on us. The Lord never left us, as we've accused him of doing. On the contrary, we've ignored him and forsaken his ways. We've taken him for granted, making him into a mere mortal, like ourselves. That's why we've become an easy prey for our enemies. We've brought all this distress upon ourselves, because of our disobedience and idolatry.

"I know our holy Lord smites entire nations for disobeying his word. How can I now disobey his call to go against Baal's army? The Lord means what he says. And if he has declared that I have might, then I'm going to believe him. He also said he would go with me, and I know his covenant promises can't fall. So, I'll gladly go."

Please note here – Gideon didn't have the peace to go forward until he acknowledged he was dealing with a righteous, holy God. The revelation of Jehovah Shalom – the Lord, our peace – was given to Gideon only after he cried, "Alas, O Lord God." He was confessing, "Oh, Lord, I regret, grieve, sorrow and repent that I didn't acknowledge you as almighty God." Then, in the exact moment Gideon recognized and honored the God he was dealing with, the Lord revealed himself as Jehovah Shalom. The very next verse reads, "The Lord said unto him, Peace be unto thee; fear not: thou shalt not die" (Judges 6:23). God was saying to Gideon, "I'm Jehovah Shalom the Lord, your peace." At that point, scripture says, "Gideon built an altar there unto the Lord, and called it Jehovah-shalom" (6:24).

Here's another lesson I believe the Lord wants to teach us through this story:

Shalom – God's peace – is a gift from the Lord.

Shalom cannot be earned. Nor is it given to everyone who claims to be a Christian. Tragically, multitudes in the church today do not have shalom. Like Israel, many believers have experienced only short seasons of peace between their lengthy periods of distress. They often quote the words of the Lord: "Peace I leave with you, my peace I give unto you: not as the world giveth, give I unto you. Let not your heart be troubled, neither let it be afraid" (John 14:27). "Now the Lord of peace himself give you peace always by all means" (2 Thessalonians 3:16). Yet, as Judges shows, it's impossible to receive the Lord's shalom until we deal with God according to his various attributes.

How else can we honour the Lord as God almighty, unless we deal with him as he really is? We know he's omnipresent, everywhere at once. And he's omniscient, all knowing. He's also omnipotent, all powerful. Moreover, he's merciful, kind, patient, long-suffering, compassionate, full of love and grace. He's all of these things – yet he's much more. God is also holy, just, pure, severe, unchangeable, a despiser of sin, no respecter of persons. The apostle Paul writes soberly of these latter attributes: "Behold therefore the goodness and severity of God: on them which fell, severity;

but toward thee, goodness, if thou continue in his goodness: otherwise thou also shalt be cut off" (Romans 11:22).

I believe many Christians in this current generation have no revelation of the almighty God with whom we have to deal. Such casual believers have rejected the God of Acts, who slew two members of a Spirit-filled church because they lied to the Holy Ghost. They've ignored the God who refuses to forgive those who won't forgive others. And they don't believe in the God who states he'll mercilessly judge all who refuse to show mercy to their brothers. Here is a God, Paul says, whose wrath "is revealed from heaven against all ungodliness and unright-eousness of men, who hold the truth in unright-eousness" (Romans 1:18).

As I look back over my life, I recall many times of distress, trouble and restlessness. I see now that during such times, I had no power to stand against the enemy as I should have. And I realize why I lacked God's peace for seasons at a time, even though I had a genuine love for the Lord. The fact is, I simply didn't see the Lord as a holy, just God. I ignored all the scriptures about his wrath and justice. Instead, I focused only on those passages having to do with his love and mercy. I was unknowingly rejecting the severe God and accepting only the gracious one.

I also see that in those times of distress, the Lord was urging me to deal with certain strongholds in my life, such as my temper. But I wasn't willing to face those things. I didn't want to deal with them righteously. Now, like Gideon, I look back on those times and cry out, "Oh, Lord – I took you for granted. If only I'd known who you were. If only I'd understood not just your mercy and grace, but also your holiness, your justice, your righteousness, your wrath against sin."

How dare we continue to sin willingly and casually in God's presence? How dare we sit in his house singing, praising, appearing to be righteous, when all along we're gossiping, slandering our brothers and sisters, committing gross sins? How dare we continue living double lives instead of fearing God's wrath and discipline? How dare we seek justification for all our evil doings? If only we knew whom we were dealing with, we would cry out as Gideon did, "Alas, my Lord and my God. Woe is me – I'm sinning before the holy, righteous judge of all men."

We'll never receive the Lord's shalom until we realize, "This is serious business. This is God almighty I'm dealing with, creator and sustainer of the universe. How can I continue taking him for granted? Why do I still test his grace, living with this lust as if he's deaf and blind to my secret acts? Why can't I see that I'm indulging all these habits before a righteous judge who means what he says about his holiness?

"Oh, Lord, I'm grieved by my sin. I realize I've tried to serve you while still holding onto my idol. I've treated you as if you were someone weak, like me. And I've doubted what you've said to me in your word. I've questioned your love and leadings.

Please, father, forgive me. Open my eyes, and reveal your holy God-ness to me."

Do you tremble at God's word? Are you ready to obey everything it says? If so, you'll receive the revelation of Jehovah Shalom. He'll come to you personally as "the Lord, your peace," filling your spirit with supernatural strength against every enemy. You can't earn this kind of peace; it's a gift from God. Nor can you work it up. It comes to you only when you recognize and honour the one you're dealing with: almighty God, holy and righteous.

When Gideon received the revelation of Jehovah Shalom, he had to be comforted by this thought: "He is truly God almighty – high, holy and righteous. Yet, didn't he just come to me in mercy? Didn't he approach me in pure love? Yes, he's holy – but this holy God made the first move toward me. He took the initiative. He came to me in my doubt, laziness and disobedience. Of course, he had every right to cast me aside. But instead he offered me power, might and clear direction. The Lord came to deliver me, not to damn me."

That's what the cross is all about. Jesus came to you in your sin, and that ought to bring hope, joy and peace to your heart. He had every right to cast you aside. But instead, he came to you speaking deliverance, empowerment, courage and valour.

Make no mistake – the Lord didn't choose Gideon because he saw something great in him. No, he revealed Jehovah Shalom to Gideon as a gift. And today the Lord makes this same offer to us. He's telling us, just as he told Gideon, "I'm about to send you forth to do battle against your enemy. But don't worry. I'm going to send you out with my peace filling your heart."

Our response should be like Gideon's: "The Lord says I'm a person of courage and valour. And I know he's a holy God who cannot lie. Therefore, no matter how I feel, no matter how I may be discouraged by my past sin, I'm going to trust what my Lord has said to me. He has commanded me to go, so I'll go."

Now you can go forward with Jehovah Shalom – the Lord, your peace – because he has given it to you.

6

Jehovah Tsidkenu
"The Lord Our Righteousness"

"Behold, the days come, saith the Lord, that I will raise unto David a righteous Branch, and a King shall reign and prosper, and shall execute judgment and justice in the earth. In his days Judah shall be saved, and Israel shall dwell safely: and this is his name whereby he shall be called, THE LORD OUR RIGHTEOUSNESS" (Jeremiah 23:5-6).

Most Christians today hold a common concept of righteousness. As we understand it, being righteous means embodying a combination of the following traits: uprightness, morality, virtuousness, good conduct, avoidance of all evil and fleshly temptations.

We all know believers who embody these wonderful traits and more. In every apparent way, they love God and his church. They're faithful to the Lord's work and to fellowshipping with his people. And nothing in their lives can be pointed out as being unrighteous. They're faithful to their spouses. They don't smoke, drink, curse or carouse. They don't cut corners on their job or cheat on their taxes.

And they don't allow themselves to defile their hearts by feasting their eyes on filthy videos, movies or TV.

Such people are kind, considerate, gentle, soft-spoken. They never gossip or speak against others. Instead, they say only good things about people, including those who despise them. In short, they walk a good, straight path of faith, in purity of heart. As we consider their example, we can't help but think, "There goes a righteous man. There goes a righteous woman."

Yet there's a fundamental problem with thinking of righteousness in this way. You see, you can possess all of these wonderful qualities – you can do every good thing and be upright in every way – and yet still be no more than a good person in God's eyes. In fact, all of these traits can be the result of hard work to establish a righteousness of one's own. Indeed, it's possible for us to arrive at this kind of moral, upright life through a fierce struggle of our flesh. We can attain all the human graces – we can be morally clean, turning aside from everything that's of flesh and the devil – and still fall infinitely short of righteousness in God's eyes.

For example, I've met many non-Christians who are very good people. They're meek, kind and loving. They'll do virtually anything to help anyone. Yet they aren't righteous at all, by God's definition. Sadly, the same is true of many believers. They're dedicated servants who pray diligently, read their Bibles often, give their entire lives to ministering to the poor and the needy – but they know little of being righteous by biblical standards.

I grew up in a branch of the Pentecostal church that emphasized a legalistic approach to being righteous. This brand of Pentecostalism involved struggling and sweating in the flesh to obtain holiness. In recent years, God has opened my eyes to all that he is and wants to be to his people through the New Covenant. And today, I grow sad as I recall the hardships many Pentecostal people put themselves through over the years. Some believed the only way they could be righteous was to fast for forty days and nights. Yet very few people could actually do this. Many ended up cheating their way through an intended fast, their consciences condemning them. And it all happened because they were desperate to keep up an appearance of righteousness.

I know that many earnest readers of this book have fought valiantly to rid themselves of besetting lusts and habits. They've striven for years to crush the dominion of sin in their lives. I've known this struggle myself. I know what it's like to want to be an overcomer more than anything else in life (see Revelation 2:7, 11, 17, 26; 3:5, 12, 21; 21:7). And yet I know what it's like to fall far short with every attempt.

I know the awful struggle of trying to break free from a stronghold, of hating a particular sin that refused to let go. I know the guilt, the tears, the self-hatred I've experienced whenever I've been defeated by that sin. And I know the endless cycle of confessing my sin, making promises to God, striving to do better, sweating it out one more time to try to attain righteousness. Then, finally, just at the point I thought I'd made it – that I'd overcome my sin and achieved a measure of holiness – I fell back into a temptation that broke my heart all over again.

Each time, I ended up going to my prayer closet and weeping before the Lord. I got so frustrated, I even yelled at God: "What do you want from me, Lord? How can I ever reach a place in my life that's pleasing to you? You know I only want to be right-eous. I've tried everything – yet I fail at every turn. Why can't I ever attain righteousness?"

In my opinion, very few people in the church today have a true understanding of righteousness. And yet the understanding of Jehovah Tsidkenu – the Lord our righteousness – is absolutely crucial to the church's survival in these last days. Lately, my soul has been so gripped by what I see coming on the earth, I can hardly find words to express it. Christians are going to need the very righteousness of God himself to make it through.

I believe we're going to see an apostasy such as the church has never known – a falling away more widespread than anything we could imagine. Hell is going to spill over its borders with unspeakable evils. The world will be besieged by lusts and temp-tations so seductive and powerful, untold multi-tudes of Christians will be overcome. Pleasure madness will engulf our children. And we'll see a moral collapse so overwhelming, it would cause us to faint if it were described to us today.

In 1974, I wrote a prophetic book called *The Vision*. In it, I described the beginnings of this overwhelming flood of sin. Already we're seeing many of those prophecies come to pass. I devoted an entire chapter to the phenomenon of video pornography, in which people would be able to pipe X-rated movies into their homes. Keep in mind, I wrote this long before the advent of VCRs or cable TV. Readers at the time were shocked at the idea; they thought it could never happen. Yet today, people are not only able to bring X-rated videos into their homes, but they're able to see nudity on prime-time television every night.

Right now, our society is being drowned by a tidal wave of lust, yet we don't even know it. The Internet is yet another purveyor of pornography into the home. Teenagers and young children are able to pipe porn into their own bedrooms through their computers. Granted, the vast majority of information on the Internet is good, but 90 percent of user activity on the Internet involves pornography.

If the church is going to survive the coming moral landslide, we're going to need a proper revelation of righteousness from God's point of view. And we're going to have to know how to obtain his righteousness. If we don't grasp this revelation of Jehovah Tsidkenu – if we don't understand the Lord our righteousness – we're going to be swept away with the rest of the world, in utter despair and anguish.

God gave the prophet Jeremiah a revelation of Jehovah Tsidkenu in a time of crisis similar to the one we face today.

The godly prophet Jeremiah lived during the reign of King Josiah. You may recall that Josiah was a righteous king, a man who walked humbly before the Lord. You may also remember that one hundred years before Josiah's ascension to the throne of Judah, the sister nation of Israel had been dispersed and taken captive. During that period, God had hoped Judah would learn from Israel's mistakes. But the people of Judah refused to look at their own sin. In fact, Judah and Jerusalem fell into sin that was worse even than Israel's. The Bible says Judah became so corrupt, God finally couldn't endure it any longer. In his eyes, the nation's wound was beyond curing: "There was no remedy" (2 Chronicles 36:16).

Of course, these people lived under the Old Covenant, which required perfect obedience. So when Josiah took the throne, the godly king tried to bring about righteousness in Judah by imposing morality on the people. He did this through government decrees and military enforcement. And, under Josiah's leadership, a revival took place in Judah. Idols came down, evil was wiped out, and the people's conversations focused on the Lord and his work.

Yet this revival was an outward one only. It wasn't a genuine revival of the heart. It was also a shallow revival, full of good works and appearances but not accompanied by true repentance. The people of

Judah observed the law and cleaned up their society
– but their hearts weren't in it. This became evident
later, when Josiah died in battle. At that point, Judah
fell back into gross wickedness. And within a year,
the people were indulging in idolatry such as the
nation had never seen.

Jeremiah was overwhelmed by what he saw taking
place among God's people. Soon adultery and
homosexuality had become rampant. The prophet
cried, "The land is full of adulterers; for because of
swearing the land mourneth; the pleasant places of
the wilderness are dried up, and their course is evil,
and their force is not right" (Jeremiah 23: 10).

Even Judah's priests and prophets had become
corrupt. In turn, they corrupted God's house: "For
both prophet and priest are profane; yea, in my
house have I found their wickedness" (23:11). These
religious leaders should have been warning the
people about God's judgment for their sin. They
should have been faithfully pointing out the difference between the holy and the profane. But instead,
they comforted the people in their sins. Jeremiah
listened in disbelief as these false teachers preached
peace and prosperity to evildoers, encouraging
them in their backsliding: "They say still unto them
that despise me, The Lord hath said, Ye shall have
peace; and they say unto every one that walketh
after the imagination of his own heart, No evil shall
come upon you" (23:17).

Judah's condition became so awful that God
compared them to Sodom and Gomorrah, two cities
he'd wiped off the map:

"Wherefore their way shall be unto them as slippery ways in the darkness: they shall be driven on, and fall therein: for I will bring evil upon them, even the year of their visitation, saith the Lord. And I have seen folly in the prophets of Samaria ... I have seen also in the prophets of Jerusalem an horrible thing: they commit adultery, and walk in lies: they strengthen also the hands of evildoers, that none doth return from his wickedness: they are all of them unto me as Sodom, and the inhabitants thereof as Gomorrah" (23:12-14).

Jeremiah could only weep as he saw Judah totally overrun by gross immorality. He cried, "Let mine eyes run down with tears night and day, and let them not cease: for the virgin daughter of my people is broken with a great breach, with a very grievous blow" (14:17). Finally, the prophet delivered a message of coming judgment: "(God) will now remember their iniquity, and visit their sins" (14:10).

The similarities between conditions in Judah and those of our day are astounding.

At the time Jeremiah was prophesying judgment, Judah had enjoyed nearly forty years of prosperity. The Lord had honoured King Josiah's attempts to bring revival to the land. Yet, even so, a sword of judgment had hung over Judah all that time. You see, God had already predetermined to send his wrath upon the nation. Why? He wouldn't forgive the bloodshed of innocents committed by the previous generation. Josiah's predecessor, evil King

Manasseh, had murdered multitudes of innocents, filling Jerusalem's streets with blood.

Scripture tells us God will not pardon the shedding of innocent blood in any society: "Surely at the commandment of the Lord came this [judgment] upon Judah, to remove them out of his sight, for the sins of Manasseh, according to all that he did; and also for the innocent blood that he shed: *for he filled Jerusalem with innocent blood; which the Lord would not pardon*" (2 Kings 24:3-4, italics mine).

God declared of Manasseh's sin, I will not forgive this sin, ever." Indeed, never in history has God withheld his judgment from a society that has shed great amounts of innocent blood. London was destroyed because of its bloodshed in the seventeenth century. And the Roman Empire fell because of the innocent blood it spilled throughout the centuries.

I believe America is next. How can God withhold his wrath from our nation, which has shed the blood of 35 million innocent babies through abortion? Each day in this country, 5,000 unborn children are killed. The Lord has raised up prophetic voices in America, to cry out warnings of judgment. And many Christians gather in meetings across this country to pray for our nation. But God's judgment on America has already been determined. Our nation will not be spared.

I believe that right now we're enjoying a brief reprieve from God's fiery judgment. It appears our nation is prospering as never before. But the handwriting is on the wall. And the Lord is issuing one final mercy call, because he desires to see repentance.

He did the same thing with Judah during Josiah's reign. God told that righteous king, "I know you're a praying man and a godly leader. And I'm going to give your people a brief time of prosperity and peace. So, Josiah, you won't see my judgment fall on Judah during your lifetime. But after you're gone, my judgment will surely come upon this nation, for all its shedding of the blood of innocents."

In the midst of this crisis of grief and despair, God gave Jeremiah a fresh revelation of his character.

At that point, Jeremiah received a heavenly revelation of a future Jerusalem. According to the prophet, this new holy city would be ruled by a righteous branch from the seed of David: "Behold, the days come, saith the Lord, that I will raise unto David a righteous Branch, and a King shall reign and prosper, and shall execute judgment and justice in the earth" (Jeremiah 23:5).

Jeremiah adds that this branch would save his people, causing them to live in peace: "In his days Judah shall be saved, and Israel shall dwell safely: and this is his name whereby he shall be called, THE LORD OUR RIGHTEOUSNESS" (23:6). This is very clearly a prophecy about Jesus Christ, who would secure his people's salvation by his own blood and bring about the heavenly Jerusalem. Indeed, the prophet Zechariah identifies this branch as Christ – someone who "will remove the iniquity of that land in one day" (Zechariah 3:9).

Beloved, we are living in the very day when "he [Jesus] shall be called, THE LORD OUR RIGHTEOUSNESS" (Jeremiah 23:6). So, what does all this mean for us, in practical terms? What is this righteousness he's the Lord of – and how are we to know and understand Jesus in this role?

You're probably already convinced that every bit of your righteousness comes to you from God, through Jesus' work on the cross. In fact, you may often speak of Christ's righteousness being imputed to you (that is, credited to your account). You may think of your righteousness as being of faith, and not of works or law. You may even forswear trying to work out a righteousness of your own.

Yet, as much as we all may believe these truths, often they aren't worked out in our daily lives. They haven't become a reality to us in the ways that God has intended. Simply put, our lives need to be revolutionized by a revelation of Jehovah Tsidkenu. Indeed, only as we lay hold of God's concept of righteousness by faith will it become reality.

From the time of Moses through the prophets, God raised up witnesses who foretold a day when a Saviour would come and bestow his own righteousness upon a spiritual Israel.

The apostle Paul confirms this amazing truth. He writes, "Now the righteousness of God without the law is manifested, being witnessed by the law and the prophets; even the righteousness of God which is by faith of Jesus Christ unto all and upon all them that believe" (Romans 3:21-22).

Paul is telling us, in essence, "We're living under a New Testament revelation. It's the revelation of a righteousness that comes from God and not from man. The Lord chose to disclose this revelation to his Old Testament prophets. And every one of them testified of a righteousness to come, which would not be of the law. They said a messiah was coming to bestow this righteousness on man, rather than man trying to earn it by his own merits. Clearly, the prophets were foreseeing Christ's day."

By its very nature, the Old Covenant points to the revelation of Jehovah Tsidkenu, the Lord our righteousness. You see, the law was actually designed to show man the weakness of his flesh. It demanded perfect obedience. And under the law, man had to strive until he came to the point that he died to his flesh. At that point, the work of the law was complete. And the need for Jehovah Tsidkenu became clear.

David was one Old Testament witness to Jehovah Tsidkenu, the Lord our righteousness. He wrote of the coming messiah, "In his days shall the righteous flourish; and abundance of peace so long as the moon endureth" (Psalm 72:7).

Isaiah was another such witness. He wrote, "Surely, shall one say, in the Lord have I righteousness and strength: even to him shall men come; and all that are incensed against him shall be ashamed. In the Lord shall all the seed of Israel be justified, and shall glory" (Isaiah 45:24-25).

How did Isaiah receive this revelation of Jehovah

Tsidkenu, the Lord our righteousness? It came to him the hard way – through a deep, trying personal experience.

In the first five chapters of Isaiah, we see the prophet preaching faithfully and walking closely with the Lord. I'm convinced that if we had sat under this devoted man's ministry, we would have received the very mind of God. Our souls would have been pierced by sharp arrows of conviction, our lifestyles challenged and changed. By every indication, Isaiah sought God's righteousness with all his heart.

Yet the Lord gave this godly prophet an incredible vision that changed his entire view of righteousness. In this vivid revelation, Isaiah saw the Lord sitting on his throne, high and holy, lifted up above everything in heaven. The vision was so awesome, so filled with God's holiness and glory, even the heavenly seraphims surrounding the throne had to cover their eyes and bow in humility. They cried in an otherworldly voice, "Holy, holy, holy, is the Lord of hosts" (Isaiah 6:3).

The scene was so heavy with God's holy presence, it drove Isaiah to his knees. He fell face down, unable to see anything except his own sinfulness. Keep in mind, this was the same man who sought God's righteousness more diligently and preached his word more faithfully than perhaps any person on earth. Yet now this godly prophet found himself crying, "Woe is me! for I am undone" (6:5). The Hebrew meaning of this phrase is, "I've failed – I perish."

Isaiah then makes an incredible statement. He says, "I am a man of unclean lips" (6:5). How could this be? Isaiah had been preaching, prophesying, delivering a pure word from heaven with convicting power. Yet now he was so awed by what he witnessed, he called his own words unclean.

Do you get the picture? Isaiah, among the godliest of all the Lord's servants, was stating, "I can't be holy, I can't be righteous. I'll never be able to attain that. I've done the best I could – yet, at the end of it all, I've discovered I'm nothing. After all my preaching, all my seeking and searching, I'm absolutely undone by the Lord's awesome righteousness. I see clearly now, there is no good thing in me."

Isaiah realized there was no way he could ever attain true righteousness on his own. And even if he could, it would never stand in the light of God's holiness. So, what could he do now? How would he ever be able to enter into God's presence with his head lifted up?

It became clear to Isaiah he would never be accepted in the Lord's eyes unless God himself took the initiative. The Lord had to come to him in his dead condition and do the work of purging and cleansing him.

And God did just that. He directed an angel to take a pair of tongs and remove a live coal from the fiery altar (which represented Christ's sacrifice). The angel then laid the coal on Isaiah's tongue, saying, "Lo, this hath touched thy lips; and thine iniquity is taken away, and thy sin purged" (Isaiah 6:7).

What does this scene signify? Isaiah was now

accepted. He was purged and purified, and he could stand before the Lord. He was able to worship along with the seraphims, singing, "Holy, holy, holy is the righteous Lord."

God's message to Isaiah here, and to every believer today, is crystal clear: we attain true righteousness only by coming to the end of ourselves and by turning to Jehovah Tsidkenu to provide it. Isaiah's justification came by no other means than his words of confession: "Woe is me – I'm undone." He speaks for us all when he says, "In my own strength and ability, I'm helpless, unable. I can never make myself righteous. Instead, the Lord has purged me by his own blood. He did it all for me. He made me righteous, by placing that hot coal on my tongue. I've been purified by his actions, not mine. All I did was tell him I'm hopeless, lifeless, a dead man without him."

This is why Isaiah could testify, "Surely, shall one say, in the Lord have I righteousness and strength: even to him shall men come; and all that are incensed against him shall be ashamed. In the Lord shall all the seed of Israel be justified, and shall glory" (Isaiah 45:24-25).

The prophet Jeremiah was given the clearest witness of all concerning Jehovah Tsidkenu, the Lord our righteousness.

We've already seen what God revealed to Isaiah about how man attains true righteousness. Now, in Jeremiah 23:6, God deals a death blow to all self-righteousness in the coming kingdom of Christ. He declares through Jeremiah once and for all: "In his days Judah shall be saved, and Israel shall dwell safely: and this is his name whereby he shall be called, THE LORD OUR RIGHTEOUSNESS."

The Lord was saying, "The day is coming when I will send my righteous one as a savior to all who accept him. He's going to secure a people through his own sacrifice. And they'll know him as Jehovah Tsidkenu, the Lord our righteousness."

The moment God revealed himself as Jehovah Tsidkenu, he declared his utter contempt for every kind of righteousness attempted by flesh. Here in this single verse, proclaimed hundreds of years before the messiah would appear, God was declaring it a deadly sin for us to try to establish a righteousness of our own. He was saying, in other words, "You must lay down and renounce every effort to be holy through your own strength and abilities. Your Saviour alone, the coming messiah, will be your righteousness."

Even though this knowledge is revealed clearly to us in God's word, we still resist embracing it. We simply don't want to believe there is no good thing in us. We can't bring ourselves to accept that, in our flesh, we're helpless, undependable, prone to commit the vilest of sins. George Whitefield, the great eighteenth-century preacher, sums up this heart attitude when he writes, "Self-righteousness is the last idol that is rooted out of the heart."

We may testify to the world, "My righteousness is as filthy rags. I can never earn or merit favour with

God." Yet often, we still refuse to submit wholly to the Lord's righteousness. Even when we're convinced we've done this, we tend to backslide into our old striving – into the self-inflicted agony of trying to cut off our besetting sins by our own efforts and strength.

The truth is, we can never know true righteousness until we give up hope, once and for all, of ever finding anything good in ourselves we can bring to the Lord. The righteousness of God is a gift, one that must be imputed to us, credited to us. It comes to us unearned, unmerited. Indeed, the Lord must initiate the process by which we receive his righteousness. He must come to us carrying cleansing fire from his altar, to purge us and account us as being holy in his sight apart from any worth of our own.

How do we become candidates for this gift of righteousness? It happens only when we admit with true conviction, "Woe is me – I've failed. I'm helpless, Lord, finished, undone. Without you, I'm a dead man."

Now we come to the question: what is true righteousness, from God's perspective?

Paul gives us some insight into God's definition of righteousness in several New Testament passages. In each of these passages, Paul speaks of God crediting his righteousness to Abraham:

- "Abraham believed God, and it was counted unto him for righteousness" (Romans 4:3).

- "Faith was reckoned to Abraham for righteousness" (4:9).
- "Even as Abraham believed God, and it was
  accounted to him for righteousness" (Galatians
  3:6).

Each of these verses refers to one thing that Abraham
did to attain true righteousness: he *believed.*

Finally, Paul provides the Lord's definition of
righteousness: "(Abraham) staggered not at the
promise of God through unbelief, but was strong in
faith, giving glory to God; and being fully
persuaded that, what he had promised, he was able
also to perform. And therefore it was imputed to
him for righteousness" (Romans 4:20-22).

The Bible could not make this matter any clearer.
Simply put, righteousness is believing the promises
of God, being fully persuaded he'll keep his word.
Conversely, unbelief is staggering at his promises,
doubting God will do what he promised.

Paul explains, "Now to him that worketh is the
reward not reckoned of grace, but of debt. But to
him that worketh not, but believeth on him that
justifieth the ungodly, his faith is counted for righteousness" (Romans 4:4-5). Jesus himself settles this
matter of believing God for our righteousness: "This
is the work of God, that ye believe on him whom he
hath sent" (John 6:29).

You may object, "But what about the issue of
personal obedience? Aren't we supposed to deny
ourselves and reject the world? Aren't we
commanded to forsake all lusts of the flesh? And

what about taking up our cross? Doesn't the Bible say we're to continually surrender ourselves to the Lord, walking in purity and seeking a life that's pleasing to him?"

I say none of these things is possible unless we're fully persuaded God will keep his covenant promises to us. It all comes down to trusting in his word. The fact is, our acceptance doesn't depend on any of these things. We're accepted by God only because we are in Christ. You see, God accepts only one person, Jesus – and, in turn, we're accepted because we believe in his finished work for us on the cross. I repeat Paul's adamant declaration: "Now the righteousness of God without the law is manifested, being witnessed by the law and the prophets; even the righteousness of God which is by faith of Jesus Christ unto all and upon all them that believe" (Romans 3:21-22).

Go ahead – read your Bible through in a year, as a sense of duty. Pray for hours each day. Go to church every time the doors are open for services. Wrestle down your besetting sins. Be good, and do good. But, I tell you, "Without faith it is impossible to please him" (Hebrews 11:6).

Abraham demonstrated the righteousness that's of faith when he willingly obeyed God's command to sacrifice his own son, Isaac. Paul writes of the patriarch, "He believed, even God, who quickeneth the dead, and calleth those things which be not as though they were" (Romans 4:17).

The Lord watched as Abraham raised a knife to slay his son. And he heard the cry of faith in

Abraham's heart: "Lord, you pledged that this son would be my heir. You said Isaac would be the child of promise who would father entire nations. So, I'm fully persuaded that as soon as I slay my boy, you're going to raise him from the dead. I know your word cannot fail, God. I believe you're able to fulfill everything you've promised to me."

Indeed, God responded by saying, "That is the righteousness that's of faith, not of works. Abraham is my definition of a righteous man."

David also was a righteous man by God's definition. Paul writes, "Even as David also describeth the blessedness of the man, unto whom God imputeth righteousness without works, saying, Blessed are they whose iniquities are forgiven, and whose sins are covered. Blessed is the man to whom the Lord will not impute sin" (Romans 4:6-8). David knew he possessed a blessedness that was not of himself. He realized he was forgiven and accepted before the heavenly father only because he trusted in God's righteousness.

All along, the only thing the Lord has asked of his people is trust.

God's only demand of his people has been, "Believe my word. Trust in my promises. Have faith that I will do the impossible for you."

We may accept this as a doctrine of our faith and as proper theology. Yet, in practical terms, many of us still believe God expects more from us than faith. Deep down, we tell ourselves we don't pray enough, give enough, sacrifice enough. We think God expects us to be more diligent, more disciplined, more faithful. Something inside us keeps insisting, "I can't be righteous before the Lord without more effort, more pain, more struggle." So our flesh jumps in and tries to help God make us righteous. Yet all along, the only thing God has asked of us is simply to trust him to do what he has already promised.

Beloved, this is the very kind of unbelief that kept Israel out of the promised land. The Israelites' sin wasn't just idolatry or adultery. It was unbelief – their lack of faith in God's word to do for them what he'd promised.

I often read biographies of Christians whom we consider to be righteous people of faith. Many of these men and women renounced their worldly possessions, gave away their money to the poor, forsook their careers and friendships. Some chose to live in a sparsely furnished home, or a single room, or even a small hut. And they devoted their time and energy to praying, ministering or helping the poor.

I've always considered such people to be the epitome of righteousness. I've thought, "This person was a breed apart from those around him. His walk of faith appeared so spiritual, so godly, so devoted. Obviously, his is the kind of life God considers to be righteous."

Soon I began to measure my own life against these people's. I was convinced, "If only I could live the way these saints did, then my life would be pleasing to the Lord. I just need to move into a small, simple home, drive an old junker car, and get rid of all my possessions except the clothes on my back. If I do these things, then maybe I'll grow into a spiritual giant."

Yet it didn't take long for me to realize, "Even if I did these things, I could never measure up to these saints. My life is too full of failures. Those godly people were so meek, so gentle, so dedicated. I'm too far below them in this matter of holiness. I'll never reach their righteous example. It's just not going to happen for me."

Over time, I found myself weighed down by a burden of condemnation. I'm convinced multitudes of other Christians carry around the same heavy weight of guilt. They think their lives will never measure up to the standard they see exemplified by others.

Beloved, this self-condemnation is all the result of judging righteousness by outward appearances. The truth is, some of the people who led lives of sacrifice remained sinful in God's eyes. Why? They never fully trusted his word that he would be their righteousness. Instead, they relied on their own works and goodness.

God's word leaves no doubt that the Lord considered his servant David to be a righteous man. Yet if we were to judge David's life by the way we judge our own, we wouldn't think of him as righteous at all. He committed adultery, covered it up, murdered the man whose wife he slept with, then lied about it all (even to a prophet of the Lord). Think about it:

had David been a minister in our day, even the most liberal denomination wouldn't hesitate to defrock him. He brought terrible reproach upon God's name. And today his evil deeds would be splashed all over the front pages and beamed onto TV screens.

Yet David had a repentant heart. And most of all, he trusted not in his own righteousness, but in Jehovah Tsidkenu, the Lord our righteousness. David cried, "Judge me, O Lord my God, according to thy righteousness; and let them not rejoice over me ... my tongue shall speak of thy righteousness and of thy praise all the day long" (Psalm 35:24, 28).

Perhaps you're like David. You've lost all confidence in your own flesh. You're convinced there is nothing good in you to be brought to God. On the contrary, you see that all you have to present to him are your struggles and failures. And you realize that unless he accounts to you his righteousness, you're doomed.

So you've turned everything over into the Lord's hands. You're trusting him, casting all your cares upon him. And you believe in his promises to keep you, protect you and cause you to walk uprightly before him. You state, "I believe God's word. And if he says he's my righteousness, then it's his job to make it so in my life. He says his name is 'the Lord our righteousness' – and that applies to me. I may not have arrived yet, but I know it's not my job to make that happen. It is the Lord's. And I know that somehow, by his Spirit working in me, he's going to get me there."

God doesn't want your home, your car, your furniture, your savings, your possessions. All he wants is your faith – your strong belief in his word. And that may be the one thing that other, more spiritual-appearing people may lack. You may look at another person as being more spiritual than you. But that person may actually be struggling hard to keep up an appearance of righteousness. Yet, as God looks at you, he declares, "There is a righteous man or woman." Why? You've admitted your helplessness to become righteous. And you've trusted in the Lord to give you his righteousness.

Pauls tells us we're accounted as righteous in God's eyes for the same reason Abraham was.

The apostle writes, "Therefore it was imputed to (Abraham) for righteousness. Now it was not written for his sake alone, that it was imputed to him; but for us also, to whom it shall be imputed, if we believe on him that raised up Jesus our Lord from the dead" (Romans 4:22-24).

You may claim, "I believe this. I have faith in the God who resurrected Jesus." Yet, the question for you is, do you believe the Lord can resurrect your troubled marriage? Do you believe he can bring to life a spiritually dead relative? Do you believe he can raise you up out of the pit of a debilitating habit? Do you believe he can erase your cursed past and restore to you all the years the cankerworm has eaten?

Do you believe in the God who can take the nothingness of your situation and make something out of it? Do you believe he can take a vessel who's weak, foolish, uneducated – someone despised and looked down upon – and make that person useful in his kingdom, confounding others who seem wise and mighty?

When everything looks hopeless – when you're in an impossible situation, with no resources, and no hope before you – do you believe God will be your Jehovah Jireh, seeing to your need? Do you believe he's committed to keeping his covenant promises to you – and that if even one of his words fails, the heavens would melt and the universe collapse?

Scripture shows us why so many Christians give up believing the Lord for his righteousness and go back to trying to establish their own.

I'm convinced that most believers today have no patience. They may have plenty of faith, but they don't have the patience required to wait on God to fulfill his promises. Yes, Abraham's faith made him righteous in God's eyes. But Abraham also had to learn patience. Why? He was required to wait almost half a century before God fulfilled his word to him.

Of course, Abraham didn't possess this patience right away. You may remember some of his sinful actions during the long years of dryness before God's promise came. At one point, Abraham agreed

to a flesh-conceived deal his wife had made, to give
him their promised son through a maid. That
certainly wasn't an act of faith. Rather, it was a
shortcut to faith, brought on by the flesh's impa-
tience. Eventually, God brought Abraham to a place
of faith, where he inherited the promise. But it
happened only after he acquired patience.

Our great need for patience is repeated
throughout the book of Hebrews:

- "For when God made promise to Abraham,
  because he could swear by no greater, he sware by
  himself … *and so, after he had patiently endured, he
  obtained the promise*" (Hebrews 6:13-15, italics
  mine).
- "Be not slothful, but followers of them who
  through faith and patience inherit the promises"
  (6:12).
- "For ye have need of patience, that, after ye have
  done the will of God, ye might receive the
  promise" (10:36).

Beloved, God has given us many wonderful
covenant promises – to break every bond of sin, to
empower us to defeat all dominion of Sin, to give us
a new heart, to cleanse and sanctify us, to conform
us to the very image of Christ. His word assures us,
"Now unto him that is able to keep you from falling,
and to present you faultless before the presence of
his glory with exceeding joy" (Jude 24).

Yet God does all of these things for us only in his
time, according to his divine schedule. He has no

deadlines pushing him. And he ignores all demands
for an instant cure-all. In short, true faith on our part
demands that we patiently wait on our Lord. Our
response to him should be, "Lord, I believe you're
true to your word. And by the power of your Spirit
within me, I'm going to wait patiently until you
bring these things to pass in my life. My part is to
remain in faith, waiting on you."

You may endure awful trials and temptations.
And you may hear horrendous lies whispered to
you by Satan. At times, you may fall. In fact, you
may wonder if you'll ever reach the goal. But, as
you're enduring all of these afflictions, if you'll
simply hold onto faith with patience – trusting God
is at work, keeping his word, being your Jehovah
Tsidkenu – he will look upon you as righteous. He
has sworn by oath, "By faith, you will receive the
promise."

Your flesh may try to rush in and help. It may urge
you to turn back to the Old Covenant system of
works, to try to establish your own righteousness.
But you must stand firm in faith, declaring, "Lord, I
trust only you. My flesh is pulling at me, but I
believe you to bring me back to faith. You've said I
am the righteousness of God in Christ, and I believe
you to fulfill that in me. I serve Jehovah Tsidkenu –
the Lord my righteousness."

7

Jehovah Shammah
"The Lord Is There"

"The name of the city from that day shall be, The Lord is there" (Ezekiel 48:35).

The prophet Ezekiel describes a terrifying vision he was given by the Lord. In this supernatural vision, Ezekiel saw God's glory departing from both the temple and the city of Jerusalem. As the Lord's glory departed, awful judgments began to fall – on the temple, the city and all of Judah.

The prophet had been warning the people about coming judgment for many years. Now, as this terrifying vision was unveiled to him, Ezekiel knew without a doubt he was seeing the prophesied judgments begin to fall.

The vision began with the image of a nearly indescribable chariot. This chariot had "wheels within wheels" and was drawn by legions of cherubims. Evidently, the wings of the cherubims provided the physical force that moved the chariot in each direction. What an awesome sight: a supernatural chariot supported by winged creatures from heaven.

As the chariot descended from the firmament, Ezekiel saw within it a figure sitting upon a throne. The figure was brilliant in appearance – as bright as a sapphire, the prophet says. We can safely assume this figure was none other than the Lord. And the glory that Ezekiel witnessed was the Lord's manifest presence. (The New Testament tells us Jesus is the brightness and brilliance of the father's glory. And if we compare Ezekiel's description to other passages in the Old Testament in which the Lord appeared, we can be sure this brilliant figure was Christ.)

Ezekiel saw the cherubim-propelled chariot descend and hover over the temple. Now the full impact of the chariot's terrible mission began to dawn on Ezekiel: it had come to remove God's shekinah glory from the temple. The Lord was visiting his people in order to withdraw his glory from them.

Ezekiel was alarmed. Yet he knew exactly why God was removing his glory. He'd seen with his own eyes all the awful things God's people had done in the previous years, both in the temple and throughout the land. For example, in the temple's outer court, the people had turned away from the holy place. Instead, they faced east, to worship the sun. In addition, they had allowed all kinds of creeping, crawling creatures into the temple. Evidently, they had been sacrificing snakes, lizards and other reptiles, and they'd neglected to offer the pure sacrifice of lambs. Now God was saying, "I will no longer tolerate these abominations in my house. I won't allow my glory to coexist with such sin."

Ezekiel watched in horror as the heavenly chariot literally picked up the glory of God, removed it from the holy place, and carried it to the temple door. "Then the glory of the Lord went up from the cherub, and stood over the threshold of the house; and the house was filled with the cloud, and the court was full of the brightness of the Lord's glory" (Ezekiel 10:4). God's glory was on the move. Now it was poised at the door, on the very threshold of leaving the temple.

Scripture describes one final blast of God's glory – a last shining forth of his presence in the midst of the people: "The sound of the cherubims' wings was heard even to the outer court, as the voice of the Almighty God when he speaketh" (10:5).

How did God's people react to this awesome display of supernatural power? No one even noticed. The priests and people went about their business, fulfilling all their rituals and activities. How could this be, you ask? Obviously, these people were incapable of recognizing the departure of God's glory in their midst. They'd become so blinded by their fleshly pursuits, they didn't realize his presence was about to leave them.

In spite of Ezekiel's warnings over the years, Judah had grown backslidden. The nation was full of idolatry, rebellion and wickedness. The people had given themselves over to all kinds of horrible practices – sensuality, demonic visitations, perverted worship with prostitutes. And the priests had allowed false prophets to infiltrate the temple. These false guides filled the people's minds with empty hopes of peace and prosperity. Ezekiel tried to warn the people about the consequences of their evil practices. But they dismissed him, mocking his words and continuing to indulge their flesh.

Judah's blinded condition shows us it's possible for God's people to lose the Lord's presence and not know it. They'd been deceived by their own sin. This wasn't the first time such tragic deception had befallen God's people. Scripture says that when God's presence left Samson, he didn't realize what had happened: "(Samson) wist not that the Lord was departed from him" (Judges 16:20).

Why didn't this mighty man of God know that the Lord's Spirit had left him? Like Judah, he was blinded by sin. Samson openly indulged in sensuality, never thinking he would reap any consequences. He'd become convinced, "It doesn't matter what kind of lust I indulge in. I can accomplish great exploits for the Lord at any time. I can get back up every time, and do the same things for God I've always done."

I know of churches that are just like Samson. For years, their congregations have indulged in abominations, worldliness, lukewarmness, apathy. And over those years, God has withdrawn his glory from their midst. The people have no idea that their persistent sin has driven away the Lord's holy presence. Like Samson, they remain convinced, "Everything in our church is the same as it's always been." So they attend to business as usual. The engage in dry routines and rituals, merely going through the motions of their empty religion. But in

God's eyes they're spiritually dead.

It doesn't take long for praying people in this kind of congregation to recognize something is wrong. Their sensitive hearts tell them something important is missing. Finally, to their horror, the Holy Spirit reveals he is no longer in the place. He makes it clear God has removed his presence from that church, because the leaders and the people have persisted in permissiveness and compromise with sin.

The same is true of individual believers. Right now, multitudes of Christians sit in the laps of their own Delilahs, indulging in blatant disobedience to God's word. Over time, they've become deceived by their sin, just as Samson was. They think, "I'm still a servant of God. His Spirit is still with me. Nothing has changed. I can go on as I always have." They don't realize God's glory has already departed from them. His presence is no longer in their lives, because they refuse to give up their disobedience.

Ezekiel grieved as God finally lifted his glory from Judah's midst.

As God's glory hovered at the temple door, Ezekiel saw it moving once again. He writes, "Then the glory of the Lord departed from off the threshold of the house, and stood over the cherubims. And the cherubims lifted up their wings, and mounted up from the earth in my sight ... and the glory of the God of Israel was over them above" (Ezekiel 10:18-19).

The cherubims mounted an upward surge that

seemed to lift God's glory up from the temple. Next, these angelic beings rose and held the glory above the city, suspended in the sky above the people. This hovering, hesitating image suggests the Lord was reluctant to leave. He seemed to be waiting for a voice to cry as David did: "Don't leave us, Lord! Don't take your Spirit from our midst. Please, return your holy presence to us."

I imagine Ezekiel screaming in his soul as he beheld this scene. He probably wanted to shout, "Somebody, somewhere – please, get up and cry out to God. Who's willing to stand in the gap? God's glory is on the move, about to be withdrawn from you. You've got to call upon the Lord right now, before it's too late."

But there was no such voice, no outcry, no intercessor. Nobody stepped forward to stand in the gap. So God lifted his glory and removed it from Judah: "The glory of the Lord went up from the midst of the city, and stood upon the mountain which is on the east side of the city" (11:23). (The mountain Ezekiel describes here was the Mount of Olives.)

How did the people respond, once God's glory left them? You might think the priests would have shut down the temple and ceased all religious activities. You might think they would have called for a day of mourning and repentance in recognition of what had happened, especially in light of the judgments falling. But the temple doors didn't close – not at all. On the contrary, everything continued just as it always had. Once again, the priests and people went about doing all the things they usually did.

Now these sinful people could be much more comfortable about indulging their sin. They'd been miserable whenever the Lord's glory was present among them. It constantly exposed their sin. But now that God's glory was gone, conviction was gone. They didn't care a bit that the Lord had removed himself from their midst.

So it is in many churches today. Many dead congregations once enjoyed the Lord's presence in their midst. Their pastors were mighty men of prayer. They stepped into the pulpit each week armed with a pure word from God. But then a compromising pastor came in. Over the years, sin was allowed and compromise crept in. Eventually, the people closed the doors to the Holy Spirit's conviction. And now, all over the world, these congregations are dying. They've turned their eyes away from their sin. They prefer not to allow God's holy conviction to touch them. As a result, old-line denominational churches are closing down at an alarming rate.

Fourteen years into the Babylonian captivity, Ezekiel received another amazing vision.

By this time, both Israel's and Judah's spirits were utterly broken. God's people had been in captivity for fourteen years, their pride long since laid in the dust. As they slaved by the rivers of Babylon, they wept as they remembered the glory of Zion. They no longer had anything to sing about. There was nothing in their lives that they wanted to praise God for. So they hung their harps on the willows. They finally faced the fact that God had removed his glory from them years ago because they'd desecrated his house with grievous abominations.

Now, Ezekiel once again received a vision from the Lord. And this revelation was even more amazing. This time the Holy Spirit took the prophet to a high mountain overlooking Jerusalem and all of Judah. There God showed Ezekiel another city – one the Lord would build in the future. This city would be glorious beyond all imagination. In fact, its expanse would be so great, it couldn't be contained within the nation's borders.

God then revealed to Ezekiel yet another incredible vision. This one was a revelation of a great, majestic new temple. The wondrous structure would be the permanent temple to which God's glory would return and never leave.

As the Lord unfolded the revelation of this temple to Ezekiel, he gave the prophet minute details of its entire construction. He showed him its courts, rooms and chambers, and described the kind of priests who would minister in the temple. What a complex structure the temple would be. It took Ezekiel nine chapters, 40 through 48, just to outline it.

Because Ezekiel describes the temple as impossibly huge and majestic, I believe we're not to interpret it as being a literal temple. Rather, it was meant to represent the majestic kingdom of Christ.

I don't believe we're to attempt to find symbolism in every detail of this magnificent structure. Even the most astute theologians have gotten lost in a jungle of mystical allusions while trying to interpret the details symbolically. Nevertheless, many continue to try. They go to great lengths to apply specific meaning to each of the measurements Ezekiel lists about the temple's dimensions – how many cubits high, how many cubits wide, how many miles long. That's not what this vision is all about. Ezekiel was not seeing a literal temple. Indeed, there's no evidence anywhere in Ezekiel's writings to suggest this temple was intended to be an actual building.

Certain Christian groups differ on this matter. For example, some subscribe to the Orthodox Jewish interpretation that there will be a rebuilt temple, with animal sacrifices restored to worship practices. They believe that through the temple's restoration, the Jews will turn to the Lord.

In my opinion, this belief goes against everything Paul tells us in Galatians. The apostle firmly declares there was only one true lamb slain from the foundation of the world. And that lamb's sacrifice took place once and for all. In other words, all animal sacrifices we see in the Old Testament were only types and shadows. They were replaced by the reality of Christ's sacrifice on our behalf. As the author of Hebrews tells us, Jesus' sacrifice is a finished work. Therefore, because the blood of bulls and goats cannot forgive sin, such animal sacrifices are now a wasted offering.

Besides all this, why didn't the Jews ever try to build the structure Ezekiel described? After all, their

captivity eventually ended, and they returned to
Jerusalem to rebuild the temple. Yet, when this
happened, not one detail of Ezekiel's vision was
adopted. Why not? It was simply impossible to
accomplish, and the people knew it. The Jews may
once again rebuild the temple in Jerusalem, but
God's glory will not be in it unless Christ is there.

If you were to outline the dimensions of the
temple Ezekiel described, including all its environs,
it would encompass twice the land mass of Judah.
This in itself made such a structure impossible to
build. Second, how could any human being devise
the kind of river Ezekiel described – one that origin-
ated in the temple and increased in volume as it ran
outward for miles? Ezekiel said this river began at a
person's ankles, then rose to the knees, and finally
became deep enough to swim in. What human
could construct such a flowing body of water out of
the midst of a building?

It's obvious Ezekiel was seeing the Jerusalem
which is above. He was describing a holy city
coming down out of heaven, which the New
Testament calls the church of Jesus Christ. Ezekiel
was being given a vision of the New Jerusalem – the
mother of all believers, to whom the glory of God
would return and never depart. This remarkable
vision of Christ's church is strikingly similar to a city
described in Psalm 46:4-5: "There is a river, the
streams whereof shall make glad the city of God, the
holy place of the tabernacles of the most High. God
is in the midst of her; she shall not be moved: God
shall help her, and that right early."

I have no doubt Ezekiel was seeing the world-wide, spiritual city that is to be our Lord's habitation forever. This was the true temple – the body consisting of every born-again believer, a tabernacle that couldn't possibly be made with human hands.

Paul echoes this in his letters to the Corinthians. He says God's temple is embodied in our physical beings: "Know ye not that ye are the temple of God, and that the Spirit of God dwelleth in you?" (1 Corinthians 3:16). "Ye are the temple of the living God; as God hath said, I will dwell in them, and walk in them; and I will be their God, and they shall be my people" (2 Corinthians 6:16).

**I believe God is giving the church today both
a hope and a warning through what
Ezekiel saw coming.**

What can we learn from Ezekiel's vision? I believe the Lord wants to reveal two things to us:

1. The prophet envisioned the glory of God returning, as well as a people of Jehovah Shammah coming forth.
Ezekiel writes, "Then brought he me the way of the north gate before the house: and I looked, and, behold, the glory of the Lord filled the house of the Lord: and I fell upon my face" (Ezekiel 44:4). This amazing new temple was a gigantic structure, filled from one end to the other with the Lord's brilliant glory. When Ezekiel laid eyes on it, he fell on his face.

I wouldn't even begin to try to put symbolic terms to all the things Ezekiel describes in this vision. But I believe the various rooms and chambers that make up this glorious temple could represent the various peoples of the world. In my opinion, Ezekiel was seeing all the races becoming one under the roof of God's house. He writes, "The name of the city from that day shall be, The Lord is there" (48:35).

The literal Hebrew words for this last phrase are Jehovah Shammah. Ezekiel was saying, in other words, "These people will be known by God's presence in them and upon them. It will be said of this temple, 'God is there. The presence of the Lord is with them.'"

2. The Lord told Ezekiel to guard the gates to this new house, in which the glory of God would now abide.

The implications to Ezekiel were: "I will not put up with the abominations I endured in the old temple. You have to warn the people about this." We've already read of all the awful things the people brought into the temple during the old order. God said the priests during that time "ministered unto them before their idols, and caused the house of Israel to fall into iniquity" (Ezekiel 44:12). In turn, the fleshly worshippers clamoured for shepherds who would encourage their idolatry, confirming them in their sins. The result was that both ministers and lay people polluted God's house with corrupt worship.

Now the Lord was putting a stop to all of that. He

told Ezekiel, "Thus saith the Lord God; No stranger, uncircumcised in heart, nor uncircumcised in flesh, shall enter into my sanctuary" (44:9). God was instructing the prophet, "Ezekiel, I have set guards over these temple gates. And I don't want them to let any strange shepherd or ungodly person enter. No one who's uncircumcised in heart can be permitted into my holy place. I'm going to have a holy body inhabiting my last-days church. And I won't allow any polluters to corrupt this house. No one with an unclean heart can stand and minister before me."

What does this mean for us, in these last days? It means Satan won't be allowed to invade the holy temple where God's glory dwells. The Lord has proclaimed that his church's pastors and individual believers will be full of his glory. And he won't allow any ungodly, unclean person to minister in this new temple. He told Ezekiel, "They shall not come near unto me, to do the office of a priest unto me, nor to come near to any of my holy things, in the most holy place" (44:13).

You may wonder, "But there are all kinds of corruption and pollution in the church today. Backslidden ministers continue to condone the sins in their flock. Certain denominations are ordaining homosexual pastors. Church leaders are excusing adultery, mocking the reality of heaven and hell, denying the scriptures to be the inerrant word of God. How could anyone believe the church today hasn't been corrupted?"

You're right to recognize these awful abominations going on in the church. Such ministers and leaders are wolves in sheep's clothing. They're seducers, flatterers, compromised shepherds who refuse to show the people their sins. And because they don't believe in the authority of God's word, they receive no fresh word from the Lord. When they stand in the pulpit to preach, they simply repeat other men's sermons. These godless men of the cloth minister not to God, but to the idolatry and wickedness of the people. And they're causing their flocks to fall even deeper into iniquity.

I tell you, these shepherds will never minister in the holy temple Ezekiel saw coming. God has already declared that the days of mixture are no more. Therefore, all the foolishness and abominations we see going on are not a part of God's true house. These awful things are part of the old, dead order, and God has forsaken that order. He has already declared it won't be so in his holy sanctuary, where Jehovah Shammah abides.

No doubt, you've heard this common cry among concerned believers: "The church has totally lost its influence in society. It has lost all of its political clout. And it's completely irrelevant in the eyes of young people. The perception we get through the media and from our nation's leaders is that the church is merely incidental to people's lives."

If you think the carnal church has lost its power and authority on earth, you can be sure it has even less influence in heaven. The backslidden church in America today certainly has no power with God. Over the years, it has become a stench in his nostrils.

The Lord has wiped his hands of it all, refusing to have anything to do with a self-satisfied, lukewarm church. He's already written off whole demoninations, declaring, "Ichabod – my glory has departed." One day soon, he's going to spew this backslidden church out of his mouth.

There is only one church our Lord recognizes. His true temple – his holy sanctuary, where his glory abides – consists of a righteous ministry and a faithful, God-hungry people. This is not the visible, structured church system. Rather, this church is made up of a body here, a body there in Africa, India, China, the United States and other nations. In these holy houses, the uncircumcised in heart are not allowed to minister, and they never will be. Instead, God has a people who are righteous before him, and who will remain so until Jesus comes.

What is the name of this church? It's known as "The Lord is there" – the church of Jehovah Shammah.

The church named Jehovah Shammah – "God is there" – is pastored and shepherded only by the Zadok priesthood.

Ezekiel tells us the ministers in the glorious new temple will consist of an entirely new order. He describes this new priesthood by first telling us what the old order was like. God says through the prophet:

"The Levites that are gone away far from me,

when Israel went astray, which went astray away from me after their idols; they shall even bear their iniquity. Yet they shall be ministers in my (old) sanctuary, having charge at the gates of the house, and ministering to the house: they shall slay the burnt offering and the sacrifice for the people, and they shall stand before them to minister unto them. Because they ministered unto them before their idols, and caused the house of Israel to fall into iniquity; therefore have I lifted up mine hand against them, saith the Lord God, and they shall bear their iniquity. And they shall not come near unto me, to do the office of a priest unto me, nor to come near to any of my holy things, in the most holy place: but they shall bear their shame, and their abominations which they have committed" (Ezekiel 44:10-13).

In this passage, the Lord outlines all the abominations of the old order. They will continue with their rituals and programs, but God swears they will not be ministering to him, nor will they "come near him." Then, as soon as the Lord finishes, he begins to describe the new temple priesthood who will lead and serve his people:

"But the priests the Levites, the sons of Zadok, that kept the charge of my sanctuary when the children of Israel went astray from me, they shall come near to me to minister unto me, and they shall stand before me to offer unto me the fat and the blood, saith the Lord God: they shall enter into my sanctuary, and they shall come near to my table, to minister unto me, and they shall keep my charge" (44:15-16).

The Hebrew name Zadok means right or right-eous. Ezekiel is referring here to a man named Zadok who served as priest during King David's reign. This righteous man never wavered in his faithfulness to David or to the Lord. He stood by the king and by God's word, through thick and thin. It didn't matter whether David was reigning power-fully from Israel's throne or fleeing the holy city to escape an uprising led by his rebellious son Absalom. Zadok always remained loyal to David, because he knew the king was the Lord's anointed.

Not every priest had this attitude, however. Abiathar was also a priest under David's reign. When Adonijah overthrew his father and pronounced himself king, Abiathar forsook David and joined the rebellion. The ordeal revealed Abiathar's faithless heart. Later, when David's son Solomon ascended the throne, he banished Abiathar to the wilderness. He told the priest, "You have been faithless in your role as a priest unto the Lord. You no longer have any part in the temple ministry." To this day, God has nothing to do with the Abiathar church.

Because Zadok remained faithful through every-thing, he came to represent a ministry distinguished by its faithfulness to the Lord. Indeed, Zadok was a prime example of a true minister of God – separated from this world, shut in with the Lord, consistently hearing from heaven. Such a minister recognizes his main work as prayer: seeking God daily, constantly communing with the Holy Spirit and ministering to Jesus. Moreover, this kind of minister cannot be bought at any price. While other ministers chase after every new, exciting religious fad, this shepherd remains faithful to the Lord and to his priestly service in the temple.

Such is the Zadok priesthood. And the Lord has many Zadokites in his temple service today. You won't find these shepherds rushing to their pulpits from some personal pursuit. Zadokites wouldn't dare try to preach a lifeless sermonette or some message that hasn't come from God's heart. Instead, these priests come to the pulpit from their secret closet of prayer. They're faithful to stand before the Lord before they ever stand before the congregation. They spend precious hours in the Lord's presence, until they're saturated with a message that's been burned into their souls. And when they emerge from God's presence, they're able to speak straight to the people's hearts. Their message gets down to where the sheep live, because it has come directly from God's throne.

The Lord says of the Zadok priesthood, "These ministers will enter my sanctuary and stand before me. They shall come near to my table and minister to me. And they shall keep my charge. I'll be faithful to lead and direct them. And I'll give them my word for my people."

The Zadok priesthood includes every single member of this new temple.

In the new, last-days sanctuary, the Zadok priesthood knows their central work is to minister to the

Lord. This ministry includes every lover of Jesus who desires to walk in righteousness. Indeed, we see the "priesthood of believers" echoed throughout the books of the New Testament. The apostle John tells us, "(He) hath made us kings and priests unto God and his Father" (Revelation 1:6). "And hast made us unto our God kings and priests" (5:10). Likewise, the apostle Peter writes, "Ye also, as lively stones, are … an holy priesthood, to offer up spiritual sacrifices, acceptable to God by Jesus Christ" (1 Peter 2:5). "But ye are a chosen generation, a royal priesthood, an holy nation, a peculiar people; that ye should shew forth the praises of him who hath called you out of darkness into his marvellous light" (2:9).

You may not have ministerial credentials from any church body. You may never have been to seminary. You may never have preached a sermon. But you're just as called and ordained to serve in the Zadok priesthood as even the most well-known preacher or evangelist. Both Testaments make it abundantly clear: each of us is to hold the office of priest and to perform a priest's duties.

So, you're wondering, how are you to do this? You do it by ministering primarily unto the Lord. You offer up sacrifices to him – sacrifices of praise, of service, of turning over to him all your heart, soul, mind and strength. He's called you to be part of his royal priesthood. Therefore, you're to minister to others only after you've ministered to him.

This means you're not to show up at God's house each week empty and dry, hoping some message from the preacher will fire you up. No, you're to come prepared to minister to the Lord with a heart of praise. To do that, you need to be shut up with him often – in your home, on your job, everywhere. You've been set apart as his minister – a faithful Zadok priest who calls on his name regularly, trusting fully in his righteousness and not your own.

Unless you're a priest in this Zadok ministry – unless you stand before God's table daily, ministering to him – you can't be a member of the church of Jehovah Shammah. You may spend all your time supporting church activities and meeting others, needs. But unless you're a Zadok priest in every aspect of your life, all those other activities amount to nothing.

To be a member of God's true church, you must be known by the name of Jehovah Shammah. Others must be able to say of you, "It's clear to me the Lord is with this person. Every time I see him, I sense the presence of Jesus. His life truly reflects the glory of God."

Sadly, this can't be said of many Christians today. If we're honest, we have to admit we don't sense the Lord's sweet presence in each other very often. Why? The majority of Christians spend their time involved in good religious activities – prayer groups, Bible studies, outreach ministries – and that's all very commendable. But many of these same Christians spend little if any time at all ministering to the Lord, in the secret closet of prayer.

The Lord's presence simply can't be faked. This is true whether it applies to an individual's life or to a church body. When I speak of God's presence, I'm not talking about some kind of spiritual aura that mystically surrounds a person or that comes down in a church service. Rather, I'm talking about the result of a simple but powerful walk of faith. Whether that's manifested in a Christian's life or in an entire congregation, it causes people to take note. They tell themselves, "This person has been with Jesus," or, "This congregation truly believes what they preach."

Here is my point: It takes much more than a righteous Zadok pastor to produce a Jehovah Shammah church. It takes a righteous, shut-in people of God. If a stranger comes out of a church service and says, "I felt the presence of Jesus there," you can be sure it wasn't just because of the preaching or worship. It was because a righteous Zadok congregation had entered God's house, and the Lord's glory was abiding in their midst.

I have many minister friends who are godly, righteous Zadokite priests. These men are faithful to preach the pure word of God. But not all of their congregations are of this royal priesthood. In such churches, the pastor's sermons are ignored. The minister can see the apathy in the people. Few in his church are growing in Christ. And no one outside the church is getting saved. It can't be said of that church body, "Jehovah Shammah – the Lord is there."

My pastor friends weep many righteous tears over their congregations' apathy. But the truth is, there can be no life in that house without a holy

Zadok congregation who regularly minister to the
Lord in their own lives. No church can be any more
alive than the people who attend it. And dead
believers make for dead churches.

Every true shepherd of the Lord wants people to
walk out of his church saying, "Surely the Lord is in
this place." Yet this ought to be the burden not just
of the pastor, but of every Zadok priest in the house.
And that can happen only if there's a body of
Zadokites in the pews, people who come to God's
house after they've been with Jesus at home. Only
this kind of faithful believer can offer the Lord true
service, through holy hands held up in sacrifices of
heartfelt praise.

**Finally, Ezekiel shows us one special fruit of
the Lord's presence in the midst of his people.**

Ezekiel says that when God's glory is present, his
people will be taught to discern between what is
holy and what is unholy. As the Lord revealed his
vision of the new temple, he told Ezekiel: "They
shall teach my people the difference between the
holy and profane, and cause them to discern
between the unclean and the clean" (Ezekiel 44:23).
Whenever a body of godly servants seek to minister
to the Lord, God gives them eyes to see what's of the
Spirit and what's of the flesh. They recognize the
difference between the holy and the profane.

So, what does the name Jehovah Shammah mean
to us today? It means that others should be able to
say of us, "I see Christ in that person." We can no

longer try to fake God's presence in our lives. Others will simply know if he's present when they encounter us. They may not know exactly what they are sensing – but their heart will tell them, "That person is filled with Jesus."

8

Jehovah Rohi
"The Lord My Shepherd"

"The Lord is my shepherd; I shall not want" (Psalm 23:1).

We're all familiar with the 23rd Psalm. Its comforting message is well-known even among non-believers. This renowned Psalm was written by King David, and its most famous passage is contained in the opening verse: "The Lord is my shepherd; I shall not want."

The Hebrew word David uses for want in this verse indicates a meaning of lack. David is saying, in other words, "I shall not lack anything." When we combine this meaning with the first part of the verse, David is saying, "The Lord leads, guides and nourishes me. And because of that, I have no lack."

In this brief verse, David gives us yet another reflection of the Lord's character and nature. The literal Hebrew translation of the first part of this verse is Jehovah Rohi. It means "the Lord, my shepherd."

David continues to develop this idea of the Lord as shepherd throughout the rest of the Psalm. In the next verse, he writes, "He maketh me to lie down in green pastures: he leadeth me beside the still waters" (Psalm 23:2).

What an idyllic picture. As we read this verse, we envision a flock of fleecy, white sheep, dotting a tranquil, green landscape. These well-fed creatures graze on the plentiful grass surrounding them in a vast pasture. Or, they lie about on a lush, green carpet of grass, napping peacefully. Overhead, the sun is shining brightly. On the nearby hillside, a grove of tall, leafy trees blows gently in the breeze. And down below, a beautiful wood is reflected in a pool of cool, clear water.

The whole scene seems so pleasant, peaceful and carefree. Not a creature in sight has a care in the world. Why? Sitting on the plush grass of the gently sloping hillside, overseeing all that goes on below, is a shepherd. This shepherd is a picture of calm. He spends his time meditating on the Lord's blessings. Occasionally, he gazes out at his flock to make sure all is well. The shepherd doesn't hear a single cry or sigh from the peaceful fold in his care. Instead, he sees below him a contented flock of rested, satisfied sheep, creatures who fully enjoy their peaceful surroundings.

I ask you, what's wrong with this picture? Simply this: life is nothing like this image of idyllic existence. It's my sincere belief that this tranquil picture is not the image David intended to put forth in Psalm 23 – not at all.

The truth is, even the saintliest of God's people are a motley bunch. With that in mind, I want to paint for you another picture of the sheepfold David describes here. Yes, sheep are lying about in green grass beside still waters. But, according to Isaiah, this flock includes lambs that are frail, weak and unsteady. Some are barely able to walk. Others are in deep pain. A few are pregnant. Still others have to nurse their restless young.

Isaiah writes, "He shall feed his flock like a shepherd: he shall gather the lambs with his arm, and carry them in his bosom, and shall gently lead those that are with young" (Isaiah 40:11). Of course, Isaiah is speaking here of Christ, our Jehovah Rohi. Our Lord Jesus is our shepherd. And he came not to tend just healthy, strong sheep, but also those who are sick, broken, diseased and weak.

God condemned Israel's ministers because they didn't fulfill this role for the sheep under their care. This aspect of ministry was so important in the Lord's eyes, he spoke his displeasure through every major prophet:

- "The diseased have ye not strengthened, neither have ye healed that which was sick, neither have ye bound up that which was broken, neither have ye brought again that which was driven away, neither have ye sought that which was lost" (Ezekiel 34:4).
- "My sheep wandered through all the mountains, and upon every high hill: yea, my flock was scattered upon all the face of the earth, and none did search or seek after them" (34:6).
- "My people hath been lost sheep ... they have

forgotten their restingplace" (Jeremiah 50:6).
• "All we like sheep have gone astray" (Isaiah 53:6).

Note the last verse. Who is Isaiah talking about here, when he says we all have gone astray? He's talking about you, about me – about every person who belongs in the Lord's sheepfold. Don't think the prophet was exaggerating for effect. Mark it down: every sheep in the shepherd's fold has gone astray. Yet, each of us is still in the fold, because our gracious, merciful, loving shepherd has come after us and found us.

Just look around you for a moment, at all the sheep you know in the church of Jesus Christ. Examine yourself, your believing friends, your pastor, the people in your congregation. What kind of flock are you? Are you all lying down in green pastures, drinking pure, cool water? Are you all perfectly contented, healthy, happy, peaceful?

No way. You have in your midst baby believers who keep stumbling and falling. At times, you wonder if they're ever going to be strong enough to walk straight. Others are forced to carry their young. Their offspring aren't yet born again and walking on their own. Often these sincere believers are reduced to tears because of their young ones' strayings.

Others among us are sick and diseased. They've drunk polluted water from the well of some false shepherd. Still others are walking around wounded. Some were crippled by a bleeding hind leg their shepherd had to pull out of the lion's mouth. Others were crippled by evil habits and lusts. Still others among us are naked. They've been shorn, or fleeced, by false shepherds. These wicked deceivers took them for everything they had.

All of these sick, broken sheep have been brought back to the fold by the shepherd himself. Some were so maimed, disabled, hurt and disoriented, Jesus had to put them on his shoulders and carry them all the way back to the flock.

That's the role of our great shepherd. Scripture describes this wonderful trait of our Lord even more clearly:

- "For thus saith the Lord God; Behold, I, even I, will both search my sheep, and seek them out" (Ezekiel 34:11). The sheep Ezekiel describes here obviously have wandered away. Yet the Lord still calls them his sheep. And he willingly goes after them.

- "As a shepherd seeketh out his flock in the day that he is among his sheep that are scattered; so will I seek out my sheep, and will deliver them out of all places where they have been scattered in the cloudy and dark day" (34:12). Ezekiel is speaking here of sheep who have been through deep, dark passages. This is the experience of every devoted follower of Jesus. We all have faced dark times in our walk with the Lord.

- "I will feed them in a good pasture, and upon the high mountains of Israel shall their fold be: there shall they lie in a good fold, and in a fat pasture shall they feed upon the mountains of Israel. I will feed my flock, and I will cause them to lie down, saith the Lord God" (34:14-15). Here we see an image repeated from Psalm 23. Once again, the Lord tells us he causes his sheep to lie down.

- "I will seek that which was lost, and bring again that which was driven away, and will bind up that which was broken, and will strengthen that which was sick …

  "Therefore will I save my flock, and they shall no more be a prey; and I will judge between cattle and cattle. And I will set up one shepherd over them, and he shall feed them, even my servant David; he shall feed them, and he shall be their shepherd" (34:16, 22-23).

Once again, God speaks clearly about setting up one true shepherd to watch over his people. Of course, he's referring to Christ. Jesus is the good shepherd who promises to feed his flock.

Now let's turn back to Psalm 23:2: "He maketh me to lie down …"

The Hebrew phrase for maketh here means, literally, to induce or compel. In other words, the shepherd compels his sheep – that is, he makes them – to lie down. The literal meaning of this verse is, "He interrupts me to make me lie down."

Many in the flock of Christ today are ready to lie down. These sheep are sick, diseased, weary, fainting – and they know it. They're mud-stained, wounded, bleeding, hurting. They're in such bad shape that the shepherd himself has to recover them.

After he carries them back, he instructs them to lie down, and they happily comply.

Do you get the picture? When David writes, "He restoreth my soul" (Psalm 23:3), he's speaking of healing and restoration. He's describing a flock of bruised and battered sheep lying in a green valley. Whenever we're sick and hurting, bruised and wounded, our shepherd Jesus carries us to a place where we can be healed. And there, in the valley of his love, he operates on us. He binds up the wounded, strengthens the weak, brings life to the sick, renews the frail.

Sometimes, however, it's not easy for our shepherd to make us "lie down." Often, our flesh resists. We don't want to submit wholly to the Lord and be utterly dependent on his mercy and love. Instead, we tell ourselves we've got to tough it out, to sweat out our own failings and weaknesses. Rather than turning to him by faith and resting in his power and grace, we scamper off to some secluded place to lick our wounds and try to recover on our own.

As we lie there in our own dark covering, we try to figure everything out. We wonder how we ever could have gotten so muddy and become so wounded. We ask ourselves how we ever got to this place to begin with. We wonder, "Where did that temptation come from? How was the enemy able to bruise me so badly? What got me into this awful mess? I've got to do something to pull myself out."

Every one of us has had these kinds of thoughts. But the truth is, we'll never figure out our battle. This is exactly what David wants to address in

Psalm 23. He's describing a shepherd who comes after us, dwells in our midst, and causes us to lie down, while we depend on him for healing and cleansing.

Jehovah Rohi is not some benign, passive shepherd. He isn't a hireling – someone who does little more than provide food and guidance. He doesn't merely point us toward the grassy pasture and pools of water, and say, "There's what you need. Go and get it." Nor does he turn a blind eye to our needs. He doesn't run the other way when he hears our cries for help and sees us in trouble. No, he knows every pain we endure, every tear we shed, every hurt we feel. He knows when we're too weary to go another step. He knows just how much we can take. Most of all, he knows how to rescue us and bring us to a place of healing.

Our shepherd won't allow us to steal away to some secret place where we may try to nurse our wounds. He knows we'll bleed to death that way. So he comes to take us back, clutching us to his bosom, carrying us through every dark place, leading us back to the green valley where his fold lies. Once we're there, he tells us, "Lay aside all your fleshly dreams and schemes. Just lie down in my grace now. Do it in faith. This is a time for you to be restored."

I don't think I could relate to a fold of fleecy, white sheep who never face any troubles.

I wouldn't know what to do if I were part of a

flock where the sheep smiled all day long, showing off pearly white teeth. I don't know if I could handle going to a church where nobody ever cried or experienced pain. I'd go crazy if I lived among people who were never sick, never in need, never tempted, never depressed, never downcast or discouraged. If I were mixed in with that kind of flock, I'd be a complete misfit, a black sheep. And I'd be miserable, because my life isn't like that at all.

I get downcast at times. I go through periods of discouragement. I've experienced times of great confusion. Don't misunderstand; I have God's peace. But I don't carry a Colgate grin everywhere I go. Why? I've been through the mill. And often the trials of life don't make me happy.

I've preached thousands of sermons in my lifetime. I've written many books. I've worn out several Bibles in my studies. But I've also shed a river of tears. I've been up on the mountaintops and down in the valleys. I've been through times of testing, trial and sorrow. And, on many occasions, God has had to come after me. He's had to pick me up, bind up my wounds and give me a bath.

David asked, "Thou art the God of my strength: why dost thou cast me off? Why go I mourning because of the oppression of the enemy?" (Psalm 43:2). This man couldn't help wondering why he faced such trouble from his enemies. Yet David identifies very clearly what his trouble was: "This is an oppression of the enemy."

I, for one, know exactly what David was talking about. Every time I set out to do something I believe will have an impact for eternity on people's lives, I can predict what's going to happen. The devil is going to come in like a flood and seek to overwhelm me. For example, every time I plan to write a book, I have to prepare myself for the enemy's attacks.

Yet, at other times, I experience great physical and mental oppressions for no apparent reason. I believe this is just what David was going through when he wrote this verse. He'd been assailed by something inexplicable, some oppression of soul that had no clear origin. He had no idea why it was happening. That's why he asked God why he felt so cast off. Something inexplicable had overcome him, and he had no idea what to do about it.

Perhaps you've been through this. You woke up one day with a cloud of depression hovering over you. You had no idea where it came from, or why it fell upon you. You thought, "I've never felt this down or condemned in my life. Why is this happening to me now? What's going on?" You examined your heart endlessly. Yet you couldn't get to the bottom of what you were going through or why.

I believe every true follower of Jesus faces this ordeal. We know David was a true man of God; yet he was unable to explain the sudden despair that flooded his soul. Moreover, it came upon him at a time when his soul was hungering deeply for the Lord.

David was well acquainted with oppression. At various times, he'd been physically wounded, diseased in body, broken in spirit, cast off Israel's throne, driven out of Jerusalem, scattered to the hills, lost. He also was corrupted by grievous sins and powerful, overwhelming lusts. At times David was forced to wander across the land, fleeing across valleys, hiking up hillsides and hiding in caves.

But David had a caring, loving shepherd. Each time David was battered and wounded, Jehovah Rohi went after him, picked him up, and carried him to a quiet place of rest. Then the Lord made David lie down, so his soul could be restored.

God had to keep doing this with David throughout his lifetime. You see, David was one of those sheep he himself describes as lying in green pastures beside still waters. That's right: the sheep-fold mentioned in Psalm 23 was David's own flock. And this was no one-time scene for the king of Israel. It happened with David over and over.

God's sheep are no different today. Time after time, our shepherd comes after us, fetches us and takes us to a place of rest. He continually makes us lie down for a time of healing and restoration. Yet we so easily move away from the Lord's rest. We don't always hold to the truth we learn about his grace and peace. And soon we find ourselves wandering and straying all over again.

We fail to realize that the Lord's rest is like the food we nourish our bodies with daily: we can't retain its value unless we keep coming back to the table. We have to accept that being shepherded by God is a process he must take us through many times during the course of our Christian walk.

Jehovah Rohi – the Lord our shepherd – is compelling us to follow him into his rest, so that he might "shekinah" in our midst.

The Lord says in Exodus 29:45, "I will dwell among the children of Israel, and will be their God." The Hebrew word for dwell here is shekinah, meaning to abide or to settle down beside. This word signifies not just a passing presence, but a permanent one – a presence that never leaves. In short, the shekinah glory of God is not a vanishing imprint that disappears from our hearts like invisible ink. No, it's something God imprints permanently on our soul. It's his very near and eternal presence.

The picture here is glorious: Our shepherd offers to come to us in the midst of our pain and depressed condition, and to sit by our side. He promises to bind up our wounds and strengthen the parts of us that have become sick and diseased.

That's the shekinah glory of God: the abiding, everlasting presence of the Lord. And we often experience it when we're in the midst of trouble. Our great shepherd tells us, I want to restore you. And I'm going to do it by being present with you, even in the valley and shadow of death. My presence will be with you through everything the devil throws at you. Even if you try to run from me, I'm going to chase after you. And when I catch you, I'm going to take you in my arms and carry you back to my rest. Then I'll bind up your wounds and heal all your sicknesses."

Jehovah Rohi knows his sheep.

Scripture tells us the following about our one true shepherd:

- Jesus states, "I am the good shepherd, and know my sheep, and am known of mine" (John 10:14).
- Paul writes, "The Lord knoweth them that are his" (2 Timothy 2:19).
- Christ declares, "My sheep hear my voice, and I know them, and they follow me: and I give unto them eternal life; and they shall never perish, neither shall any man pluck them out of my hand" (John 10:27-28).

Simply put, our great shepherd knows who his sheep are. David was familiar with this aspect of the Lord's character, because he had experienced it personally. Throughout the Psalms, we read:

- "He knoweth our frame" (103:14).
- "He knoweth the secrets of the heart" (44:21).
- "The Lord knoweth the thoughts of man" (94:11).

David was saying, in essence, "The Lord knows what I'm really like, deep down." David realized that God knew his heart often strayed from his divine love and rest. Yet even though David knew this, he fully understood that his shepherd still loved him.

By his own admission, David was a man whose iniquities piled up so high, they went over his head.

As he faced the long list of his trespasses, David said it became a burden too heavy for him to carry (see Psalm 38:4). He stated, "There is no soundness [rest] in my flesh because of thine anger; neither is there any rest in my bones because of my sin" (Psalm 38:3).

Do these sound like the words of a healthy, fleecy-white, strong, obedient sheep? Hardly. David writes, "My wounds stink and are corrupt because of my foolishness. I am troubled; I am bowed down greatly; I go mourning all the day long. For my loins are filled with a loathsome disease: and there is no soundness in my flesh. I am feeble and sore broken: I have roared by reason of the disquietness of my heart. Lord, all my desire is before thee; and my groaning is not hid from thee. My heart panteth, my strength faileth me: as for the light of mine eyes, it also is gone from me" (38:5-10).

This was obviously the cry of a troubled man. As David acknowledged, "My sins are not hid from thee" (69:5).

Yet God knew not only all of David's evil thoughts, lusting ways, foolishness and evil tendencies. The Lord knew something else about David as well. He knew this servant had a tender, contrite heart. We see evidence of this in David's refusal to hide or excuse his sins. God knew David would always declare his iniquity and be sorry for his sin (see Psalm 38:18).

Like David, I have learned this glorious aspect of the Lord's character through experience. I've realized that God knows all of my frailties, weaknesses, jealousies, doubts and failings. Yet I've learned something else about the Lord as well. I've learned that he sees my heart. And he knows that, like David, I won't hide my sins from him. Instead, I'll confess them openly to my shepherd. How have I come to do this? I've learned that in spite of all my iniquities and failures, my Lord loves me.

Satan loves to move in on God's special people during dark times like those David experienced.

If you haven't experienced the dark, perplexing times David faced, I question whether you're leading a very spiritual life. Have you never been to the same dry place where David found himself? Have you never thought that the reason everything was going wrong in your life was because God was mad at you? Have you never feared you'd lost his favour by grieving him? If not, you must be living in some kind of spiritual la-la land.

Even Jesus experienced this kind of dark night of the soul. For a brief moment at Gethsemane, and later on the cross, an awful thought crossed his mind: "Why, father? What have I done? Why do I feel you've shut your countenance off from me? How long will you hide your face?"

I know exactly what David was going through. At times during my decades of walking with the Lord, I've thought my faith would never waver. I've been convinced I would always trust the Lord, no matter what. But then I'd be hit with a time of deep testing again. And soon the old doubts began to creep up on me.

At times our ministry has faced financial crunches. And, like David, I took counsel with my own heart. I panicked, suddenly scheming up plans to deliver our ministry from its circumstances. I started the day by planning cutbacks here, cutbacks there. Then I stayed up at night brainstorming ideas to raise funds.

I complained to everyone around me. I accused the Lord of letting me down. I almost gave up. But then, the next day, an avalanche of mail would pour in. Maybe it had been backed up at the post office for a few days. Or, maybe it had just been mailed in, even as I paced through the night, worrying and scheming. Each time this happened, I was painfully humbled, crying, "Lord, forgive me. What a dunce I am. Why didn't I trust you? Why did I ever doubt your faithfulness?"

In Psalm 119, after writing 175 "spiritually correct" verses extolling God's word and faithfulness, David makes a surprising admission.

After exalting God's word at length, David concludes Psalm 119 with this verse: "I have gone astray like a lost sheep; seek thy servant" (verse 176).

David is saying, in essence, "Please, Lord, seek me out, the way a shepherd searches for a lost sheep. In spite of all my biblical knowledge, preaching and long history with you, somehow I've strayed from your love. I've lost the sense of rest I once had in you. All my plans have failed. And now I realize I'm totally helpless. Come to me, father. Seek me out in this awful, dry place. I can't find you on my own. You must find me. I still believe your word is true."

David knew he'd strayed from God's rest. He knew the Lord's love should have been imprinted on his heart during his previous crises. But now, once again, he had forgotten about God's love for him. So he cried out to the Lord, begging him to seek out his lost servant.

Now the shepherd had come after David again. And as David heard his name called, his heart was comforted. He realized, "My shepherd knows me by name." David found himself being led down the hill into the green valley. And once he reached the green pasture below, Jehovah Rohi said to him, "Lie down now. Go to sleep, and rest your weary soul. Don't worry – I'll be at work, taking care of everything."

Now David testified once more:

- "I have trusted in thy mercy; my heart shall rejoice in thy salvation. I will sing unto the Lord, because he hath dealt bountifully with me" (Psalm 13:5-6).
- "I cried unto the Lord with my voice, and he heard me out of his holy hill. Selah. I laid me down and slept; I awaked; for the Lord sustained me. I will not be afraid of ten thousands of people, that have set themselves against me round about" (3:4-6).

It's important to note here that David's circumstances hadn't changed. In fact, scripture says the
enemies who troubled David had only increased
(see Psalm 3:1). But David had been restored to
God's love. Now he could say, "Salvation [deliver-
ance] belongeth unto the Lord" (3:8). He testified,
"No more self-made plans. No more sleepless
nights, trying to work things out. I eagerly enter into
my shepherd's love. I welcome his open arms
toward me. And I'm going to lie down in his rest.
I'm going to sleep peacefully in his unconditional
love for me."

**David knew Jehovah Rohi was his shepherd –
and the Lord is also shepherd over every
hurting, despairing sheep who has
been wounded.**

Our great shepherd loves every sheep who's gone
astray because of testings, trials, hurts and wounds.
We never dare to accuse our shepherd of abandoning us. He still walks beside us and watches
over us at all times.

Right now you may be waging a losing war
against some kind of temptation. You may be
battling a pornography addiction, homosexuality,
alcoholism, adultery, covetousness, lust. Whatever
your struggle is, you've determined not to run away
from the Lord. All around you, people try to justify
their sin. They look for alibis and make excuses. But
you refuse to give yourself over to sin's grasp.
Instead, you've taken God's word to heart.

Yet, like David, you've grown weary. And now you've come to a point where you feel absolutely helpless. The enemy is flooding you with despair, fear, lies. Perhaps you've entertained thoughts of suicide.

I urge you: don't give in to despair. Every true follower of Jesus eventually goes through what you're experiencing. It doesn't matter what your temptation may be. We all face the reality of indwelling sin. And yet we have a shepherd who loves us and comes after us.

The worst thing you can do right now is to stop turning to the Lord. Don't stop going to his house and having fellowship with other believers. And don't turn to the world. Jesus tells all of us, "Follow me." If you'll keep acknowledging him and following him up the hillside, he'll eventually lead you down the other side, to the green valley of healing and restoration.

Keep yourself in a repentant, sin-resistant attitude. Believe that soon you'll find yourself in the rest that God's love provides. Your shepherd knows everything about you, including your darkest places – and he still loves you. He knows where the green pastures are, and he's going to lead you to them. He'll come after you and call you by name. And when you answer, he'll assure you, "You have nothing to be depressed about. I'm by your side."

Perhaps you're a devoted believer who has known and experienced the deeper things of God. You may be a veteran of intense spiritual warfare. You may have ministered to others mightily in the

Lord. You may have received deep revelations of God that others have not. Yet, right now, you're going through a dark night of the soul no one could ever imagine. Nobody can relate to the awful pain you face every day, the endless anguish you're enduring. This is by far the most terrible trial you've ever experienced.

Your testing may become even more mystifying and inexplicable. But I want you to know – no matter what you're going through, the Holy Ghost wants to reveal to you Jehovah Rohi, the Lord your shepherd. You have a shepherd who wants to imprint his love on your heart. And everything you're going through is meant to bring you into the indescribable confidence that he loves you.

Jesus assured us, "I will never leave you nor forsake you." And our heavenly father – Jehovah Rohi, the Lord our shepherd – has revealed himself to us in Psalm 23. He tells us, I know you by name, and I know what you're going through. Come, lie down in my grace and love. Don't try to figure out everything. Just accept my love for you. And rest in my loving arms.

"Yes, I'm the Lord of hosts. I'm the majestic and holy God. I want you to know all of these revelations about me. But the one revelation I want you to have right now is the revelation of Jehovah Rohi. I want you to know me as your loving, caring shepherd. And I want you to rest assured I'll bring you through all your trials, in my tenderness and love."

Our circumstances may not change. But we can trust our shepherd to lead us into the green valley. It doesn't matter how awfully our enemies press in on us. The Lord has proven his love to us time after time.

9

Immanuel
"God With Us"

"Therefore the Lord himself shall give you a sign; behold, a virgin shall conceive, and bear a son, and shall call his name Immanuel" (Isaiah 7:14).

As a Christian, you've heard biblical teaching on the subject of spiritual warfare. Most such teaching centres on Paul's exhortation to the church in Ephesians 6:12: "We wrestle not against flesh and blood, but against principalities, against powers, against the rulers of the darkness of this world, against spiritual wickedness in high places."

You may wonder how and when this spiritual warfare began. We find the origin of all spiritual warfare in Genesis 3. Satan had just tempted Eve in the Garden of Eden. He had deceived her into eating the fruit from the forbidden tree. And in that very hour, God declared war on the devil. He told Satan, in no uncertain terms: "Because thou hast done this ... I will put enmity between thee and the woman, and between thy seed and her seed; it shall bruise thy head, and thou shalt bruise his heel" (Genesis 3:14-15).

God was putting Satan on notice. As unfolded by scripture, he was saying, "You've attempted to destroy my handiwork. Therefore, I decree that one day a child will come forth from a woman to be my ruler. And this child will be your enemy. You're going to injure his foot, and you'll think you've defeated him. But afterward, he'll plant his foot on your head and crush it. He's going to decimate all your power and authority. He's going to defeat you completely, destroying your kingdom of darkness."

This news must have struck Satan with terror. It probably sent him into a panic, thinking, "Will I recognize when this seed arrives? Who will this child be, the one who's going to remove all my power and destroy me? And when will he come? How can I expect to know him?"

Satan isn't omniscient. He couldn't possibly know whom God was speaking of when he referred to this seed. Of course, the devil knew of Christ before he fell from heaven. Satan was Lucifer then, a part of the heavenly councils of God. So he obviously knew the only begotten son of the father. But once the devil was cast out of heaven, he was no longer privy to God's plans. He knew nothing of the incarnation that was to come. And now, as the Lord declared war, Satan had no way of knowing exactly what was going to happen. He didn't know who the coming child would be, who his mother would be, or when she would deliver him.

Satan probably trembled when Eve gave birth to Cain, her firstborn. Eve must have believed Cain was the promised seed, because she announced, "I have gotten a man from the Lord" (Genesis 4: 1). In turn, the devil must have wondered, "Could this be the promised child, the seed who's coming as my destroyer?" I can imagine the relief he felt when Cain slew his brother, Abel. Satan realized, "This man couldn't possibly be the holy seed. He doesn't show the character of heaven, because he has committed an evil act."

Yet Satan must have felt the same panic every time a righteous man came on the scene. I wonder, what did he think when godly Enoch appeared, someone who was said to walk with God? Enoch lived for 365 years, preaching righteousness all of his days. The devil must have lived in fear with every passing year of this godly man's life, wondering if Enoch was his destroyer. Satan probably thought the same of righteous Noah, whom scripture says found grace in the Lord's eyes.

No doubt, Satan was relieved when Enoch suddenly disappeared, taken up to heaven by the Lord himself. This man couldn't have been the incarnate seed. Likewise, the devil was probably relieved when he saw Noah get drunk. In both cases, Satan could breathe a sigh of relief.

Then Abraham came on the scene. I picture Satan quaking in terror at this time. Abraham was the son of an idol worshipper, but something was clearly very special about this man. When God instructed him to pull up stakes and travel to a far country, Abraham obeyed immediately. And later, when Abraham came to Bethel, he built an altar to the Lord. After that, Satan probably kept a close watch on Abraham's movements, eyeing his every step.

The devil might have gloated when Abraham's wife, Sarah, was taken into Pharaoh's harem. Satan probably convinced himself, "Surely this isn't the woman who'll give birth to the righteous seed. Pharaoh will most likely impregnate her, and she'll give birth to a heathen son. No such child could be the holy one." Satan also probably did his best to see that Sarah was defiled in the harem. But God protected her supernaturally.

The devil might have been temporarily relieved when he heard Abraham telling half-truths to protect himself. Satan had to be further relieved when Abraham's concubine gave birth to Ishmael. Now the devil probably thought, "I know for a fact this can't be the holy seed. He's been born of a concubine." Ishmael's name means "God will hear" – but he still was not the seed.

Satan saw Isaac and many other righteous men come and go over the years. Finally, Moses prophesied that a man would come in the last days who would be like himself (By this, Moses meant he himself was only a type, or foreshadowing, of the messiah.) At that point, Satan knew his destroyer's arrival was marked for a date further into the future. So, as each of the prophets spoke of the coming messiah, the devil took note of their words. They foretold the child's place of birth and gave hints he would emerge from the tribe of Judah. Moreover, he would be born of a virgin.

Let me remind you here of a principle we learned in a previous chapter. Our spiritual warfare has never been about flesh and blood. It has always been a war between the heavenly father and the devil. God declared war on Satan, prophesying that the holy seed was coming to destroy him. And ever since that time, the devil has waged war to try to destroy that seed.

I think I know the moment when Satan got his first hint about where the seed would come from. In Genesis 17, God promised to give Abraham a seed in his old age and to multiply that seed. I believe Satan overheard this conversation. He paid attention when God made a covenant with Abraham and his seed, saying, "I'm going to give you a son, Abraham. And I'm going to make an everlasting covenant with your son. I promise that this son will be the father of many nations." God also said to Sarah, "I will establish my covenant between me and thee and thy seed after thee in their generations for an everlasting covenant, to be a God unto thee, and to thy seed after thee" (Genesis 17:7).

Of course, Isaac, Abraham's son, wouldn't be the prophesied seed. But the seed – Satan's destroyer – would come through Isaac's seed, from the seed of Abraham.

Satan knew the scriptures, and he studied them, searching every prophecy about the coming messiah.

We're aware that the devil knows the scriptures. He twisted them as he quoted them to Jesus, tempting the Lord in the wilderness. So, surely the enemy knew from Old Testament prophecies that Christ would come to earth by way of a woman's womb. And he knew that eventually this messiah would rise up to save humankind and crush his power. But the question was, which woman would the child come from? And where and when would he come?

The devil learned some more clues when he heard God's promises to David. As Nathan prophesied to David, suddenly the picture became much clearer: "Go and tell my servant David ... the Lord telleth thee that he will make thee an house ... I will set up thy seed after thee, which shall proceed out of thy bowels, and I will establish his kingdom. He shall build an house for my name, and I will establish the throne of his kingdom forever. I will be his father, and he shall be my son" (2 Samuel 7:5, 11-14).

Without question, Nathan was prophesying that God would send his own son, Jesus, to set up his eternal kingdom. And this son would be the seed of Abraham, the lion of the tribe of Judah.

Now, some believe that Nathan was referring to Solomon, David's literal son. After all, Solomon built God's house by constructing the temple in Jerusalem. But the temple Solomon built would last only a few hundred years. Eventually, it was torn down by God himself and cast aside as an abomination. Moreover, according to Nathan's prophecy, the house that God's seed would establish would last forever. Thus, it's clear that the temple Nathan refers to is the body of Jesus Christ, his church.

Another reason some teachers believe this passage

refers to Solomon is the next sentence. The King James Version says of the seed "If he commit iniquity, I will chasten him with the rod of men" (7:14). This phrasing, however, isn't the proper translation of the verse. Helen Spurrell's original Hebrew translation reads, "Even in his suffering for iniquity, I will chasten him with the rod of men, and with the stripes of the children of men." This echoes the passage in Hebrews that says we are healed by Jesus' stripes – stripes of suffering inflicted by the rod of men.

As Nathan prophesied, the devil probably knew he was getting closer to uncovering the identity of the seed. He'd heard it said that the chosen child would reign as a lion out of Judah. So now Satan turned his focus on that region and tribe. I believe this is the reason why so many mighty empires and armies marched against this tiny nation throughout history. Think about it: it was a non-strategic, arid country filled primarily with poor shepherds and a lot of sheep. There were no ores or precious metals in the hills. Of course, at one time it had been a land of milk and honey. But during the period we're talking about, Judah had been struck by severe famines. And at other times, it had almost been destroyed. So, why would such great kingdoms as Egypt, Babylon and Assyria come up against this insignificant nation?

The answer is simple: the devil was waging these wars. He wanted to kill the seed, to drive it from the face of the earth before it could destroy him. Satan himself was behind these pagan kings, possessing them, driving them, directing them to go after tiny Judah. Satan's one goal was to enter into this small nation and bring down its rule. He wanted to kill Judah's king and set up his own ruler. Then he could inhabit a human pawn, ruling and reigning over the tribe to monitor its every movement.

This brings us to our text in Isaiah 7.

This chapter reveals one of Satan's most overt attempts to implement his evil plot against Judah. In one hellish swoop, the devil decided to invade Jerusalem, destroy Judah's king, and set up his own man on the throne. Isaiah 7 describes a very real war, yet it also reveals a powerful type of spiritual warfare we face today.

Satan prompted two evil kings to attack Judah. These two kings were named Rezin and Pekah, pagan men who "went up toward Jerusalem to war against it" (Isaiah 7:1). We see Satan's designs against Judah in the pact these two men made together. Rezin and Pekah determined to join forces to "go up against Judah, and vex it, and let us make a breach therein for us, and set a king in the midst of it, even the son of Tabeal" (7:6).

Judah's king at the time was Ahaz, an evil man. But Satan was terrified of Ahaz just the same, because he was from David's lineage. The devil decided this man had to be slain; otherwise, his lineage would produce the destroying seed to come. So Satan went on the attack. He was convinced he could use Rezin and Pekah to march into Jerusalem, take Ahaz captive and put his own king on Judah's throne.

We know that Jerusalem, God's holy city, is a type of the church. It represents the kingdom of God in our hearts, where King Jesus sits enthroned, ruling and reigning in us. So, in this scene in Isaiah 7, we're seeing a type of satanic attack on the enthroned Christ in our hearts.

Under the devil's direction, Rezin and Pekah mounted a massive, overwhelming attack against Judah. They quickly overtook a city called Elath. Then the two kings spread their armies out over the land, overflowing the nation's cities. By chapter 7, they had already taken a major portion of Judah.

If you don't think this was a well-planned, Satan-directed war, consider the Hebrew names of the two kings. The name Rezin means "to open the eyes, the senses." And Pekah means "good, pleasurable." Where have we read these terms together before? We recognize them from the Garden of Eden, where Satan tempted Eve: "The tree was good … pleasant to the eyes, and a tree to be desired to make one wise … and the eyes of them both were opened" (Genesis 3:6-7). Undoubtedly, Rezin and Pekah represent the powers of darkness, descending on Jerusalem to destroy it.

At first glance, it appears God himself directed the two pagan kings' attack against Judah. Scripture says, "The Lord began to send against Judah Rezin the king of Syria, and Pekah" (2 Kings 15:37). Yet this verse doesn't mean God literally directed these evil men. It simply means he didn't stop Satan in his plans. Make no mistake, the Lord knew exactly what the devil had in mind. But he also knew Satan's scheme was going to be in vain.

Satan wanted to destroy not only Ahaz but also the women and children of Judah. He wanted to wipe out even the slightest chance that the seed of Abraham might come to power. In addition, the man whom Satan intended to put on King David's throne was called "the son of Tabeal." In Hebrew, this name means "almighty idol, deity."

After most of Judah had been taken, Rezin and Pekah came together outside Jerusalem. Now they were going to launch a massive onslaught against the city of God. Here we see the enemy bearing down on God's people, with every force in hell behind him. Jerusalem's leaders trembled when they heard that a great, confederated army was poised to wage war against them: "The heart of his people, as the trees of the wood, are moved with the wind" (Isaiah 7:2). Everyone wondered, "Who will protect the house of David? What will happen to the promises God made to our former king? Is the seed in danger?"

God had already made an ironclad promise to his servant David: "The Lord hath sworn in truth unto David; he will not turn from it; of the fruit of thy body will I set upon thy throne" (Psalm 132:11). The Lord was telling David, in short, "There will always be one of your seed, one of your sons, on the throne." It's clear to us today that God was speaking of the kingdom to come through Jesus. Christ himself, the seed of David, would occupy that throne.

But now the house of David was in total panic. So God's Spirit came upon Isaiah to bring forth a word to King Ahaz. The Lord told Isaiah, "Go to Ahaz at the upper gate. You'll find him inspecting the city's water supply. I want you to give him this message: 'Ahaz, you see the armies coming upon you. They have a plan to set up their own king in the midst of Jerusalem. But you're not to panic. Thus saith the Lord – their schemes will never come to pass.'"

"Take heed, and be quiet; fear not, neither be faint-hearted for the two tails of these smoking fire-brands, for the fierce anger of Rezin with Syria, and of the son of Remaliah. Because Syria, Ephraim, and the son of Remaliah, have taken evil counsel against thee, saying, Let us go up against Judah, and vex it, and let us make a breach therein for us, and set a king in the midst of it, even the son of Tabeal: Thus saith the Lord God, It shall not stand, neither shall it come to pass" (Isaiah 7:4-7).

Isaiah found Ahaz just where the Lord had told him. The king was inspecting the water conduit outside Jerusalem's walls, to make sure nothing disturbed the city's drinking supply when the enemy arrived. Here we see a picture of a man trusting totally in his flesh. Ahaz had already sent a delegation to Assyria's king, to try to hire his army to save Jerusalem. Ahaz had paid a price, in silver and gold, to try to obtain a defense against the two kings.

So, was God's promise to David truly in jeopardy?

Was the lion of the tribe of Judah actually in danger? Not according to what God had prophesied to Isaiah. The Lord was saying, essentially, "These two kings are like firebrands. They may look fierce, red-hot and flaming, but I have totally taken the fire out of them. Now they're nothing but smoke. Their plan against you isn't going to work, Ahaz. Just be quiet, be still and trust in me."

Sometimes it looks as if the same two smoking firebrands, called principalities and powers, will prevail in our time.

Today, Satan's smoking firebrands have also invaded our planet. And the devil has already won some great victories. He has overtaken large portions of our society – poisoning TV and the Internet, overwhelming our cities, pouring out a flood of iniquity against God's people. I can assure you, these attacks are about one thing: the devil is out to dethrone King Jesus in your heart. You don't have anything he wants except the Christ in you. He wants to depose the Lord in your heart and enthrone himself as ruler of your life.

The furious onslaught we see taking place in America today ultimately has nothing to do with politics or culture. It all has to do with the body of Christ. At times, it seems the enemy is winning many important victories in our personal war against sin. He has many believers trembling, thinking they're helpless, viewing their struggle as hopeless.

Isaiah's prophetic words apply to us just as much today: "Be careful – take heed – don't panic. Be aware of the situation going on around you. Be educated about it, by knowing God's word and being attentive to the Holy Spirit. Don't let your heart grow faint. Satan may think he's going to dethrone Christ in you and set up his own rule. But the Lord says it's not going to happen. He simply won't allow it to come to pass, if you trust wholly in him."

Isaiah was telling Ahaz he had nothing to fear: "As for King Rezin, his power is in its death throes. Within sixty-five years there won't even be a nation left of his people. They're going to be totally wiped off the face of the earth. I'm telling you, Ahaz, these kings are nothing but smoke. The Lord has put out their fire. They're powerless. Don't you understand? These men aren't your true enemy. God sent me here to tell you this isn't the real war. It's just a skirmish. The real war is farther along, way down the line. God says this battle in front of you is already over, finished. So, you have nothing to fear. Your throne will continue, if you'll just believe that he'll establish it."

Isaiah then gave Ahaz a clear warning from the Lord: "If ye will not believe, surely ye shall not be established" (Isaiah 7:9). The prophet explained to the faithless king, "The house of David and his seed are going to be established by faith alone. You have to believe God will be true to his covenant oath."

All along, Isaiah had known that Ahaz was trusting in the flesh. He was fully aware the king had relied on the arm of man, as well as his own skill and wit, in-putting together the deal with Assyria.

Here we see two distinct ways in which God's people believe they'll be delivered from Satan and his snares. First, there's the way Isaiah exhorted Ahaz: "Believe, and surely you will be established." This is the way of faith, the way of trusting fully in the covenant promises of God. But second, there's the way Ahaz went – that is, turning to the power of flesh. This is the way of human ability – of calling upon "King Willpower" to come and save you, rather than your true deliverer, King Jesus.

Maybe Satan's principalities have brought such an intense spiritual warfare upon you that you've become ensnared by a sinful habit. No matter how hard you've prayed, you haven't been able to find victory. So now you're sending your flesh out to do battle with the enemy. You're trying to make a "payoff", by relying on your own human strength.

It will never work. Why? God isn't interested in giving you victory over a single sin. The Lord is after more in your life than merely one lust or habit. He knows this isn't just a one-time battle. He sees the ongoing spiritual warfare your enemy constantly brings against you. And he wants to give you a victory that will establish you for the long term. He wants you to be able to say more than simply, I once had this sin in my life, but now I've overcome it. Instead, he wants you to be so totally established in your faith in him, you know that absolutely nothing can destroy Christ's rule in your heart. That way, when the enemy comes against you, overwhelming you with massive attacks from hell, you won't have to waver like a tree in the wind.

This is just what God wanted to do for King Ahaz and Judah. Even though Ahaz was a wicked king, and the people were disobedient and half-asleep in their faith, God still protected them. The reason God kept pressing Ahaz was because he still loved him. Though this sensual king was far from the Lord, God would not relent in trying to persuade him to turn aside from his ways of flesh and put his trust in him.

God urged Ahaz, "Ask thee a sign of the Lord thy God; ask it either in the depth, or in the height above" (Isaiah 7:11). The Lord was extending an incredible invitation to Judah's wicked king. He was saying to Ahaz, "Your faith is weak. But I want you to ask me for a sign – any sign, miracle or wonder, from heaven down to hell. I want to do a wondrous work for you, to birth true faith in your heart."

You may be shocked that God would make such an offer to any human. Perhaps you're thinking, "Didn't Jesus say only an evil generation seeks after a sign? Didn't he say there was just one sign – himself?" Yes, Jesus did say that. And I believe Christ was the very sign God wanted to show Ahaz. The Lord wanted to reveal his saving, delivering power through a miraculous work of his own faithfulness. Indeed, as we look closer, we see that this passage is all about Jesus.

But Ahaz refused to ask God for such a work. Why? He had already committed to trusting in his own wisdom. And he tried to disguise his fleshly decision as one of godliness. "Ahaz said, I will not ask, neither will I tempt the Lord" (7:12). The wicked king was saying, "I refuse to tempt God. I would never ask him for a supernatural sign. That wouldn't be holy." Ahaz had put on a robe of self-righteousness. And he couched his flesh in high-sounding, pious religious language.

How did the Lord answer Ahaz? He told him, "Therefore the Lord himself shall give you a sign" (7:14). God said, "So, you won't ask for a sign? Well, I'm going to give you one anyway." Here was the sign from the Lord: "Behold, a virgin shall conceive, and bear a son, and shall call his name Immanuel" (7:14). The name Immanuel means "God with us."

It was clear to both Isaiah and Ahaz that this prophecy had nothing to do with Judah's present battle. The word God delivered here was obviously about an event that would be fulfilled sometime in the future. Ahaz must have been baffled by this. Why would the Lord give him a sign that apparently had nothing to do with the war before him? He probably complained to Isaiah, "You're prophesying of a deliverer who might not come for years. What about this present war, our present danger? What possible good could this prophecy be to us right now?"

I believe God's purpose in speaking this word to Ahaz was simple. He was assuring the sin-blinded king that if Jerusalem still existed in the future, then the battle before him now meant this was not the end of Judah. God was giving his people then – as well as his church today – a very clear message:

"Is your faith so weak you can't believe me for this present battle? I'm going to tell you something that will build up your faith for every battle, now and in the future. There is coming to earth an Immanuel, 'God with us.' Why do I tell you this? I want you to know Judah will still be standing in the future. And, if your nation is still here when Immanuel arrives years from now, then you don't need to worry about this present battle. You're safe, Ahaz. I'm telling you: in the future, Immanuel is going to sit on the throne you're sitting on now, ruling and reigning. This is the throne of David. And I'm not going to allow anyone to harm it.

"Therefore, Ahaz, the battle you see before you isn't the real battle. It's just a minor skirmish. Satan will never prevail over Judah. He's not going to set up his throne in Jerusalem. I simply won't allow it. So, I've already declared this war before you to be over, before it has even begun."

And so it was. God blew away those two approaching powers. His message through it all was simple: "If you'll trust me, you'll never be in any danger. I'm going to make sure the throne is established. Therefore, lean on me, instead of on the arm of your flesh."

The final war was coming, and it would begin when the prophesied virgin would bring forth a son whose name would be called Immanuel.

Matthew echoes Isaiah's prophecy of Immanuel, the child to come: "Behold, a virgin shall be with child, and shall bring forth a son, and they shall call his name Emmanuel, which being interpreted is, God with us" (Matthew 1:23). This passage also names who the child would be: "She shall bring forth a son, and thou shalt call his name Jesus: for he shall save his people from their sins" (1:21). Immanuel's name is Jesus, meaning in full, "Jesus is God with us."

When "that seed which is Christ" arrived, there was no mistaking the event. Satan couldn't possibly have missed the time, place or arrival of the promised child, Jesus. There could be no question about it because it was announced from the very heavens. Angels proclaimed it from the skies: "He has come." Wise men came from afar to see him. Shepherds gathered from the hills to worship him. And he was named Immanuel.

At this point, Satan knew his warfare was no longer just a skirmish. Now he knew exactly who the chosen child was: Jesus. Yet God protected the Christ child from the enemy. He hid him away in Egypt, where Satan didn't know his whereabouts. I remind you, the devil is not omniscient. The only thing he knew was what was revealed in scripture, that the promised child would come out of Bethlehem.

After Christ arrived, Satan used Herod to slaughter every male baby in the area, hoping the promised child was among them. The devil then spent thirty-three years trying to kill Jesus. When the Lord was about to begin his public ministry, Satan tried to destroy him by urging him to leap from the roof of a temple. Throughout his life, our Lord was continually confronted by the enemy's attempts to kill him.

Finally, the powers of hell thought their hour of triumph had come, at the cross. When Jesus was killed, all of hell must have had a jubilee. Satan and his demonic powers were probably convinced, "He's dead now. We've finally killed him. That's it, the end of the battle. So much for the seed. We've won." But three days later, hallelujah! Jesus rose from the grave. The seed was alive and well.

What a surprise that must have been to Satan. Just as God foretold in the Garden of Eden, the devil had only succeeded in bruising Jesus' heel. The poison hadn't worked after all. And now that the heel had returned, he had utterly crushed the enemy's head. King Jesus was now on the throne. Christ, the seed of David, had defeated Satan once and for all, vanquishing his principalities and powers. And today, we look forward to the day when God will cast the enemy into a lake of fire for good, to be tormented forever.

What does all of this mean to us today?

Christ is in glory, safely removed from all harm by the enemy. Yet we are still here on earth, engaged in spiritual warfare with the devil and his principalities and powers. What does it mean, exactly, that Jesus has defeated Satan and given us the victory?

When we talk about the devil being defeated, we're referring to his goal of destroying the seed.

The enemy can't touch Jesus now, because Christ sits at the right hand of the father in glory, beyond Satan's reach. Therefore, that battle is over, finished. The enemy can never reach his ultimate goal of destroying Christ, the seed. All the prophecies from throughout the centuries have been fulfilled, and Satan has lost the war. In this sense, Jesus has taken away all of the devil's power against him.

Yet we also are the seed. This includes everyone who has enthroned Jesus as Lord and saviour in his heart and mind. We're Christ's own seed – his body, still here on earth. And when Jesus ascended to glory, Satan declared war on his earthly seed. So, the enemy is waging war once again; only now the battle is over the hearts of God's people. The devil's strategy hasn't changed. He's still attempting to march into the New Jerusalem – that is, into our hearts – to unseat Christ and enthrone himself as ruler over our lives.

Revelation tells us Satan would send a flood after the woman to try to destroy her. We see this happening all around us today. A flood of iniquity has been poured out on the earth, in an effort to destroy the seed. And hellish principalities are still waging war. The evil Pekahs and Rezins we face today have but one goal, one desire: to kill the seed, his beloved bride. Their intent is, "I'm going to destroy Christ's body here on earth, one by one. I'm going to poison his heel and bruise it."

Have you crowned Jesus as Lord and king of your body, soul and spirit?

Does Jesus sit on the throne of your heart? Does he rule your life as head, directing your every action and decision? If so, the hordes of hell have marked you as a target for warfare. As surely as Satan came against Judah, he'll also come against you. He'll throw at you all the weapons in his arsenal – temptations, trials, despair, discouragement. And he does it because he's after one thing: he wants to weaken your faith and trust in Immanuel. His goal is to get you to drift away from the lordship of Christ.

Right now, you may find yourself standing in satanic floodwaters up to your neck. You've been flailing frantically, doing your best just to keep from drowning. But you're afraid you soon may go under. That's exactly what happened to Judah in the book of Isaiah. Here is what the prophet cried out:

"Now, therefore, behold, the Lord bringeth up upon them the waters of the river, strong and many, even the king of Assyria, and all his glory: and he shall come up over all his channels, and go over all his banks: and he shall pass through Judah; he shall overflow and go over, he shall reach even to the neck; and the stretching out of his wings shall fill the breadth of thy land, O Immanuel" (Isaiah 8:7-8).

Consider how the Lord answered Judah's enemies: "Give ear, all ye of far countries: gird yourselves, and ye shall be broken in pieces; gird yourselves, and ye shall be broken in pieces" (8:9). Isaiah proclaimed, "Take counsel together, and it shall come to nought; speak the word, and it shall not stand: for God is with us" (8:10).

Isaiah's bold words apply equally to the church of Jesus Christ today. The prophet is telling us, "Let Satan and all his demonic forces make their plans. Let them hold meetings and consultations. All their plots and schemes are going to fail. They can never overthrow Christ from the throne of his seed."

I believe the enemy sends certain messengers from hell to buffet us. This was true in both the Old and New Testaments. The Old Testament identifies the King of Persia as a spiritual entity – a demonic force who withstood the angel Gabriel, causing a battle that lasted for days. Likewise in the New Testament, Paul speaks of evil intelligences in the spiritual realm that do battle against us.

I imagine the devil and his cohorts holding hellish counsels to plot their warfare against us. This evil empire is made up of captains, authorities, masters of many kinds of demonic devices – all under Satan's direction. They put their heads together to strategize their attacks, aiming especially at anointed servants who have subjected their lives totally to Jesus' lordship. They're determined to bring down every godly preacher of the gospel, every lay worker, every sincere believer who has enthroned Christ in his heart. If you're such a servant, you can know a hellish strategy is being formed against you right now, inside the gates of hell.

Once these evil spirits agree on their plans, they rise up and arm themselves with demonic weapons. They fill their quivers with poison arrows, laced with malice, hatred and gossip. Then they draw their swords and begin sharpening them with anger, revenge and murder. They dip their knives into the poison of despair, confusion and discouragement. Finally, Satan sends them off on their assignments, to make war against the seed.

I picture these evil warriors going forth full of pride and arrogance, confident they're going to bring down the kingdom of God. Their war cry is, "Destroy the seed, take the throne." They're determined to march straight into the holy Jerusalem of your heart, topple King Jesus from his reign there, and prepare the throne for Satan to be set upon it.

No doubt, these evil powers are assigned to individual believers' lives. The New Testament tells us that one such power was assigned to Paul. I believe the same is true for every Christian today. The devil sends forth numerous evil spirits from his war council, instructing them to tempt and trouble us, to flood our hearts with loneliness, guilt and despair.

I imagine, for example, Satan sending one of his fiercest captains to torment a dear elderly sister in Christ I know. This woman is a ninety-two-year-old prayer warrior who attends our church. She isn't well known in our congregation, but she's feared in hell because she lives only to please Jesus. The demonic entity assigned to her has been told, "She's your assignment. Now, go and dispatch her."

Even as we consider hell's war councils against us, we have to remember what Isaiah prophesied: "The enemy shall be broken and his weapons destroyed. The Lord will smash him into pieces. All of his counsel, plans and assignments will fail. Jesus Christ shall never be dethroned. If you'll simply believe, you shall be established" (see Isaiah 7:4-7).

I would love to look in on those war councils when hell's warriors return from their assignments.

After waging war, these demonic principalities have to report back to the devil. And as they return, there is no more war cry, no more enthusiasm, no more pride or arrogance. Instead, these warriors walk into the council room with their heads hanging. They've been beaten, scarred, crushed, and they're licking their wounds. Their weapons have been taken from them, broken and obliterated. All their plots have been brought to nothing.

The entity assigned to the elderly woman of prayer whimpers, "I thought she would be an easy assignment. So I nicked her with a poisoned arrow of fear. I whispered into her ear that she was going to die soon. Immediately, I saw the effects of my attack. For a few hours, the woman was discouraged. She doubted whether God was going to take care of her. At that point, I thought she was finished. I was convinced I'd gotten through.

"But then that little old woman got on her knees. She cried out, 'Immanuel, please, help me. Come and deliver me.' And suddenly, *he* appeared. He touched the poisoned spot where I'd nicked her. And in the blink of an eye, she was healed. Then he grabbed my quiver of poisoned arrows and emptied it. He broke all the arrows and tossed them aside like toothpicks. At that point, he looked me in the eye – and the next thing I knew, I was on the ground with his foot on my neck. He rubbed my face in the ground and sent me fleeing.

"Before I left, he gave me a message for you, Satan. He said, 'Take heed – Immanuel lives here. Put your warriors on notice. This woman is not alone. If you come around here again, you'll have to deal with Immanuel, God with her.'"

Another entity raises its head and laments, "I was the messenger assigned to buffet the apostle Paul. I did everything I could to that man, to try to bring him down. I tell you, nothing worked.

"I beat Paul, shipwrecked him, threw him into the ocean, slandered him. I turned the whole world against this man. I pulled out every weapon in my arsenal, using everything on the list. At one point, I thought I'd left him for dead. But as I turned to walk away, I heard Paul preaching louder than ever.

"So I had him thrown into prison. But while Paul was praying and worshipping in chains, the Immanuel Christ appeared. He unlocked Paul's bonds, opened the prison doors and sent the apostle out preaching stronger than ever. Then Immanuel picked me up and cast me out. He told me that everything I did to Paul was in vain, that it only made him a stronger warrior.

"Please, I can't go back on assignment against Paul. Every time I try to follow the apostle, I see Immanuel with him. And the more I try Paul, the more he turns to Jesus. I beg you, Satan, send someone else."

You'll never be aware of all the times an evil entity
has been assigned to attack you. Those hellish principalities are bent on tempting you, trying you
beyond your limits, destroying your faith. But,
unbeknown to you, every one of those spirits has
been sent back to the kingdom of darkness defeated,
injured and shamed. Immanuel withstood them.
And all you did was trust in him. You believed God
was with you, to fight your battle – and he did it. He
drove them all away.

Now all of hell knows Jesus is on the throne of your
heart. The devil has been soundly defeated; he knows
he can't touch Christ's throne in you. And every
power in hell is aware that Immanuel is with you.

If Immanuel is with you, who can
harm you?

Picture a Christian man who has been delivered
from pornography. He has enjoyed a year or so of
consistent victory over his former habit. Then one
day he walks by a video store and sees tapes in the
window that stir up his old lusts. The demonic
entity assigned to him is aware of his old weakness.
And now he comes against that saint with every
weapon in his arsenal. He lures the man toward an
X-rated video, and the man picks it up and takes it
home.

Imagine the report this evil messenger brings back
to Satan. He tells the adversary, "For half an hour
this man feasted his eyes on pornography on his
video player. His old lusts were inflamed. But then,

out of nowhere, he began crying out, 'Oh, Jesus, help me.'

"That's when it happened. Suddenly, the man leaped out of his chair, ejected the tape and tore it apart with his bare hands. Then he walked through his apartment shouting, 'I'm free, I'm free.'

"I thought I had him, Satan. I thought he was finished. But Immanuel showed up when he called. And I was tossed out on my head. God was with this man."

God never forsook that man for a single moment during his trial. Immanuel, King Jesus, was with him the whole time. He was with him in the video store, on the way home, and in his living room when he watched the video. And, faithfully, Jesus came when his broken servant cried out, "Help me, Lord."

This is to be our victorious confession as well, over all fear and temptation: "Immanuel is with me at all times, in my every waking and sleeping hour. God made an oath to me. He said that if I believed Immanuel I would be established, immovable, impregnable. And I believe he's with me – abiding in me, walking alongside me, protecting me. Therefore, if God is with me, who can be against me?"

That is God's desire – to have a people who'll trust him with all their trials, temptations and victories. He wants them to be totally established in their faith in him. Even wicked Ahaz and Judah were delivered and rescued from their war. But because they trusted in their own flesh, they were eventually disciplined. (Again, it isn't enough to win a single battle against hell's powers.) Yet, by grace alone, God faithfully preserved the Davidic throne of wicked Ahaz. He preserved backslidden Judah, because he'd made a covenant with their fathers.

Won't the Lord also preserve the throne he has set up in the hearts of his righteous people? Won't he also keep his covenant oath with those who love and trust in him? We alone can cast Jesus from the throne of our hearts by doing despite to his grace, turning it into lasciviousness and ending in destruction.

Therefore, we are to trust in Immanuel, "God with us." No matter what temptation, trial or fiery weapon from hell you may face, you can rest assured in his faithful hands. He has made an oath to his people. And he's faithful to keep it.

10

His Name Is Forgiveness
"The God Who Pardons"

"Who is a God like unto thee, that pardoneth iniquity, and passeth by the transgression of the remnant of his heritage? He retaineth not his anger for ever, because he delighteth in mercy. He will turn again, he will have compassion upon us; he will subdue our iniquities; and thou wilt cast all their sins into the depths of the sea" (Micah 7:18-19).

How is our Lord distinguished from all the other gods worshipped throughout the world? Of course, we know our God is above all others, set apart in every way. But one clear way we know the Lord to be distinguished from others is by his name: the God who pardons. Scripture reveals our Lord as the God who forgives, the only God who has the power to pardon sin. "Who is a God like unto thee, that pardoneth iniquity?" (Micah 7: 18).

We see this name of God confirmed throughout the scriptures:

• Nehemiah declared, "Thou art a God ready to pardon, gracious and merciful, slow to anger, and

of great kindness, and forsookest them not"
(Nehemiah 9:17). The proper translation of the
phrase "a God ready to pardon" is "a God of
propitiation" or "a God of forgiveness."

Nehemiah was speaking here of the disobedient
Israelites. Even in their rebellion against God's
word, the Lord didn't forsake his people. Instead, by
his actions he said, "My people were disobedient,
but my nature is to pardon. Forgiving isn't just
something I do – it's who I am. I'm merciful, a God
who pardons. And I won't turn my back on my
people."

• Moses asked the Lord for a revelation of his glory.
  He wasn't allowed to see God's face, but the Lord
  did reveal his glory to Moses through a revelation
  of his name. Scripture says, "The Lord descended
  in the cloud, and stood with him there, and
  proclaimed the name of the Lord" (Exodus 34:5).

What was the name of God that was revealed to
Moses? it was this: "The Lord God, merciful and
gracious, longsuffering, and abundant in goodness
and truth, keeping mercy for thousands, forgiving
iniquity and transgression and sin" (34:6-7).

Here was the name that God wanted his children to
know him by. The Lord was saying, in other words, if
you want to know who I am, and what I'm all about,
this is it. Here is my glory – that I forgive all sin, iniquity and transgression. You ask for a revelation of my
nature? Here is how I want you to know me."

- David gives us the same Hebrew description of
  God. He writes, "For thou, Lord, art good, and
  ready to forgive; and plenteous in mercy unto all
  them that call upon thee" (Psalm 86:5). David
  calls God good, ready to forgive, overflowing
  with mercy. And he penned these words out of his
  own difficult personal experience.

After sinning against the Lord, David sank into a
deep depression. He was gripped with terror
because of his iniquity. He described the experience
as being "in the depths." David spent many days
when he actually despaired of life. Finally, out of
this despair, David cried to the Lord: "Out of the
depths have I cried unto thee, O Lord ... if thou,
Lord, shouldest mark iniquities, O Lord, who shall
stand?" (Psalm 130:1, 3).

Through the testimony of these three men –
Nehemiah, Moses and David – we see three
different revelations of the pardoning nature of our
God. Nehemiah proclaimed the Lord's forgiving
nature through a prophetic revelation. Moses
described it through a revelation given to him by the
Lord himself. And David wrote of God's mercy and
forgiveness through his own personal experience
with it.

David was like many Christians today. He was a
faithful, devoted believer. He served the Lord
gladly. But at one point, he fell into grievous
sin. Afterward, he had a sense that God was
marking down his iniquities. The phrase to "mark
iniquities" means to hold or reserve our failures so

that eventually we have to face God's wrath and punishment for them. David couldn't escape the nagging feeling that the Lord was keeping a close record of each one of his transgressions.

David knew he would never survive such judgment. And now he cried, in essence, "God, if you're going to judge me by the law, I don't stand a chance. I've failed on every point of it. If you're keeping a record of my failures – stockpiling them, so I have to face them at the judgment – I'll never make it. I have no hope. I'm already condemned. If you mark our iniquities, Lord, who can stand? Who can be saved, since we all have sinned? All of us are condemned."

Suddenly, the Holy Ghost brought David out of the depths of his despair. How did he do this? He gave David a revelation of who God is. David declared triumphantly, "But there is forgiveness with thee, that thou mayest be feared" (130:4). David had been delivered from his terror by a revelation of God's name: "Our Lord forgives. His name is forgiveness." And in that moment, David's despair was lifted.

Where had David's despair come from? It came when he thought God was mad at him. He was convinced the Lord was against him because he'd failed, sinned, committed grievous acts. But the revelation God gave David was, "You'll find forgiveness with me, so that I may be feared."

What did David mean by this last phrase, "that thou mayest be feared" (130:4)? He meant simply this: the fear of God doesn't come from thinking there's a sword hanging over our head, waiting to fall on us when we stumble or fall. True fear of God comes from knowing we can serve him in peace because our sins have been blotted out. It is to revere him for his loving kindness and readiness to forgive.

David was saying, in other words, "Lord, I was ready to faint because of my sins. I was on the brink of giving up. But then you revealed your forgiving love to me. Before, all I could see was you marking my sins. Now, all I can see is you forgiving my sins and blotting them out. Finally, I can go back to worshipping you. I can serve you again. I can obey you with honor and godly fear."

Discovering the Lord as a God who forgives is the only way out of all our depths of despair, all the casting down of our souls brought on by guilt and condemnation.

Here is the key to obtaining relief from guilt and condemnation. We're to believe with all our being that our Lord is a God who forgives our sin. Indeed, this is the only power that can quiet a guilty, accusing conscience.

Most Christians are persuaded they know all about God's forgiveness. Yet so few believers live in the power and enjoyment of this amazing gift. They may know about forgiveness doctrinally, quoting chapter and verse of all the major passages concerning it. But they don't enjoy God's forgiveness experientially, as an ongoing, daily part of their Christian walk. Why?

In spite of all we've been taught about God's mercy about the victory of the cross, being ransomed by Christ's blood, being freely accepted by grace alone – the majority of us still live with uncertainty. Many believers have a nagging sense of God's displeasure. Their conscience is in constant turmoil. On Sunday mornings, they're able to teach about God's grace, preach about it, sing about it, but they never fully enjoy it. What they see in the Bible about the Lord's forgiveness simply isn't realized in their hearts.

Such Christians haven't entered into what Paul calls the "blessedness" of knowing that your sins aren't imputed against you (see Galatians 4:15). How does this blessedness manifest itself? It comes as a peace that settles our souls, because we know we have nothing to fear on Judgment Day. No matter how we may feel, or what lies the devil may throw at us, we're confident there's nothing against us in God's books.

I ask you – when the enemy comes at you with lies, filling you with fear and driving you to despair, what do you do? How are you able to combat him? I can assure you, the only way to deal with the guilt and condemnation that accompanies your sin is to be armed with a true biblical understanding of forgiveness. This kind of understanding is especially needed in these last days, as Satan's temptations become even heavier. I believe our generation is going to experience attacks from hell with more power and intensity than at any time in history. Already we're seeing new and exotic kinds of temptations, such as the flood of pornography, greed and covetousness on the Internet. And these temptations will only get worse.

Why don't many Christians enjoy the peace and rest found in forgiveness? Why haven't they laid hold of that "blessedness" Paul refers to? Why do they continue to strive, always filled with fear and condemnation? Why can't they escape their depression and despair?

It's because their conscience is thundering inside them. Every time they sin, they come under a cloud of fear that thunders the law at them. Whenever we fail God's law in any way, the conscience always pronounces wrath and anger upon our soul. That is the very purpose of our conscience. If you've seared your conscience, it will excuse you. But the conscience of a spiritual person will do what it has been designed to do by God himself. And its voice will not let up: "You've sinned – you're guilty. And now you must be judged. You have to pay the penalty for your sin."

The conscience has two mandates from God: to condemn both sin and the sinner. Here is how I see the conscience having dominion over these two territories:

1. First, the Lord has entrusted the conscience to condemn sin. And our conscience is faithful to expose to us the deceitfulness of sin. It shows us how vile sin is. And it rightly shows us that God cannot abide sin, any sin. It sees what the mirror of the law shows you.

2. Second, God has entrusted the conscience to condemn the one who sins. If you've sinned – disobeyed God's law and broken his command-ments – your conscience brings condemnation on you. And it informs you that there will be a time when you must give an account.

This is why we feel condemned when we sin. Our conscience condemns us on every point where we break God's law. And the conscience knows nothing of forgiveness. It simply hasn't been mandated to do that work in our lives. If you could ask your conscience to tell you about forgiveness, it would answer, "That's not my job. God has instructed me to expose to you the wickedness of your sin and to condemn you for committing it. That's all. Therefore, my job is to come to you when you sin and disturb your peace. I'm to tell you that what you've done is grievous and will ruin you. I'm to constantly remind you that God hates sin, and that he's going to judge it. And I'm to show you that you won't get away with your sin. God sees everything that you do in secret. And he'll make you give an account for it."

Our conscience won't move to the left or right on any point of the law. It tells us the truth about God's commandments: "Do this, and live. If you fail, you'll die." In this sense, the conscience is like a sentry. It has a post, with strict orders to man that post, and it won't swerve from its duty. Another soldier may come by and say, "Listen, the war's over. Put down your armour and celebrate." But the conscience always remains in place. It answers, "I'm not going anywhere until I hear from the captain. My job is to stay right here and keep a close watch. I won't move unless I get orders from the top."

If we're honest, we all recognize the work of our conscience in our lives. I know that whenever I sin – when I'm tempted and I fail – I descend into the depths that David described. I'm plagued with guilt. And I'm filled with terror at the thought of standing before Christ as my judge. I'm disturbed, troubled, with no peace or rest in my mind, soul or body.

Yet my conscience is only doing what it has been assigned by God to do. It's condemning me for my iniquity, putting guilt on me for having committed the sin. It's whipping up condemnation in me, because I'm guilty of having disobeyed God's word and breaking his law. All of this is meant to produce in me a knowledge of my need for pardon and restoration.

Even the God-mandated animal sacrifices in the Old Testament couldn't quiet the conscience. God's people were never delivered from the "conscience of sins" (Hebrews 10:2). Hebrews tells us, "In those sacrifices there is a remembrance again made of sins every year" (see 10:3). The conscience still had dominion to condemn both the sin and the sinner. And the Israelites' consciences continually cried out, "You're guilty."

But under the New Covenant, the blood of Christ did what no other blood sacrifice could do. At the cross, with the very first drop of Jesus' blood, the fountain of God's forgiveness opened. And out of

Calvary came the cleansing, sanctifying blood that every follower of Christ has trusted in for two thousand years. At the cross, Jesus' blood stripped the conscience of its rights and duties to condemn me as a sinner. So, now, because of God's forgiveness, my conscience no longer has that mandate in my life.

Of course, my conscience has retained its right to condemn the sin in me. In fact, that power only increased at Calvary. So my conscience is even more active in this area. I now see my sin as being increasingly vile and grievous to the Lord. And I abhor my sin more than ever. Indeed, I find myself agreeing with my conscience about my sin's deceitfulness and about God's wrath against it. Yet I thank the Lord for giving me a conscience that hasn't been seared. And I can honestly say I want my conscience to keep exposing my sin and revealing it to me as exceedingly sinful, so I can bring it to the light and repent of it.

Likewise, your conscience has greater authority than ever to reveal to you your sin's exceeding sinfulness. The difference is, your conscience can remind you of your sin – but it can no longer condemn you. You're now under the blood of Jesus Christ. Therefore, your conscience can no longer make you tremble. It can't put any condemnation on you.

However, the conscience doesn't want to let go. It will try to keep condemning you. But Christ's blood has all power to quiet your conscience. His cleansing blood tells the conscience, "I'm what you've been waiting for. You're hearing from your captain now, so stop condemning. The war is over on this particular battlefield."

Every time the devil parades some past sin before you, you may still feel condemned about it. When this happens, you have to turn to your conscience and say, "Be quiet – I'm under the blood for that sin. I repented of it, and it can't be brought up to me again. Yes, it was ugly and evil. And if I ever commit that sin again, I want you to keep showing me how exceedingly sinful it is.

"But you can no longer condemn me for it. And I no longer have any guilt plaguing me over it. God's word says there is no condemnation toward anyone who's in Christ Jesus and who walks not after the flesh but after the Spirit. Therefore, by the blood of my saviour, I'm forgiven. I have trusted in his name – in the God who pardons.

"I realize that you, my conscience, are constantly aware of sin's power. But I'm now free from your power to condemn me over past sins."

A perverted concept of forgiveness is prevalent today.

In many churches, God's mercy and forgiveness are the only topics ever preached from the pulpit. The pastors state, "God is good. He's all about mercy. And he has forgiven us all." Yet these ministers preach God's mercy and forgiveness without ever mentioning repentance or allowing their congregants to repent.

The people in these churches have never experienced a genuine soul-shaking by God's living word.
Nor have they listened to the voice of their
conscience. It isn't allowed to rightly point out their
sin and reveal the severity of God. Therefore, the
Holy Ghost isn't permitted to allow the law to
complete its convicting work in them.

Instead, the people appropriate forgiveness
without ever facing their sin. They never see how
exceedingly vile and wicked their sin is. As a result,
they end up thinking of God as being like themselves. In their eyes, he's a doddering old grandfa-
ther who overlooks the sins of those who merely do
their best.

You can see the error of these people's ways
revealed in their lives. They have no desire to do
battle with their sin. They're never stirred or moved
to give up their iniquity. And they have no desire or
hunger to become more like Jesus. They're not led to
mortify their sin through the power of the Holy
Spirit.

These people have appropriated a false peace.
And in many cases, they have seared their
conscience. They don't want to do any
soul-searching. They don't want to be troubled by
their sins or deeply convicted over them. All they
want is immunity from hell. So they've choked off
the convicting work of the Holy Ghost, working in
tandem with the conscience. The Bible states that
such people convince themselves, "I have peace,
though I walk in the stubbornness of my own
heart." Scripture also describes them as "turning the

grace of our God into lasciviousness" (Jude 4).

Things are much different in churches where true forgiveness through repentance is preached. The result there is greater obedience, more passionate devotion, and an ever-increasing love for Christ. Yet, show me a Christian who's not deeply convicted by his sin, and I'll show you someone who has no revelation at all of the meaning of biblical forgiveness. You never find this person digging deeply into God's word. He's never drawn toward the closet of prayer. Instead, he's cozy with the world. And he doesn't show any kind of deep desire or love for Jesus.

Now let's look closer at the meaning of this particular name of the Lord, the God who forgives:

1. God's forgiving name was revealed by the institution of animal sacrifices.

All of the blood sacrifices in the Old Testament were meant to teach God's people about the Lord's forgiving nature. Each of these sacrifices had to do with propitiation and atonement, which means forgiveness.

Of course, no animal sacrifice could take away a person's sin and offer total pardon. But these sacrifices did foreshadow the future taking away of our sins. Every such offering pointed to the lamb of God, who would come as a sacrifice to take away the sins of the world. At God's appointed time, his own son, Jesus, would give his life as an offering. And afterward, the people of God would stand under Christ as their banner of forgiveness.

Leviticus 16 shows us one of the most solemn of all sacrifices in Israel: the sin offering. God had instituted this event. And throughout it, he meant to explain something of his own nature and character to his people. The entire ceremony was about his readiness and willingness to forgive.

For this occasion, God called together all the tribes of Israel to gather before the tabernacle. Then, in front of the entire assembly, two goats were brought forth. These animals were presented to the Lord at the door of the congregation as an offering for sin. One of the goats was to be sacrificed on the altar. The other was to serve as the scapegoat that would carry away the people's sins.

As the first goat was led to the outer court to be sacrificed, the second goat was held outside by an able-bodied man. After sacrificing the first goat, the high priest approached the second goat and laid his hands on it. Scripture describes the scene this way:

"When he hath made an end of reconciling the holy place, and the tabernacle of the congregation, and the altar, he shall bring the live goat: and Aaron shall lay both his hands upon the head of the live goat, and confess over him all the iniquities of the children of Israel, and all their transgressions in all their sins, putting them upon the head of the goat, and shall send him away by the hand of a fit man into the wilderness: and the goat shall bear upon him all the iniquities unto a land not inhabited: and he shall let go the goat in the wilderness" (Leviticus 16:20-22).

Do you get the picture? All of Israel stood watching as the high priest placed his hands on the goat's head and began confessing the people's sins. I imagine the priest saying the following, in so many words: "I lay all the sins of this people on the head of this animal – all disobedience, all adultery, all covetousness …" When the priest finished praying, the strong man who held the goat then led the animal away, toward the outside of the camp.

At this point, I see God's people parting on either side, making a way for the goat to come through. They watch solemnly as the animal is led out of their midst. Finally, it crosses the boundary of the camp. Then the strong man leads it over a hill and into the distance, far beyond the people's sight. It is being taken into an uninhabited land, to a deep ravine with no way out for the goat. That way, the animal could never come back and haunt God's people by causing them to remember their sins. (This illustrates the word that Micah spoke to God's people: "Thou wilt cast all their sins into the depths of the sea" [Micah 7:19].)

Can you imagine what happened next? As the goat went over the hill, a shout went up from the people: "There go our sins! There go our sins!" What joy there must have been among God's people on that day.

Please understand, the Lord himself instituted this ceremony. And God's people were bound by his commandment to observe it. So, for the next 4,000 years, the Lord spoke a clear message through these sacrifices: "I am the God who forgives all sin." He was declaring to the whole world, as well as to his people: "I am forgiveness. And when I forgive you, I remove your sins from my sight forever."

You probably realize, the two goats in this cere-mony represent our Lord Jesus. He came both as the perfect sacrifice and as our scapegoat – offering his life in exchange for ours, and taking away all our sins. The Bible tells us God laid on his own son's head the guilt of all our sins: "The Lord hath laid on him the iniquity of us all" (Isaiah 53:6).

So, do you doubt God's forgiveness? If so, you need to have your own solemn assembly. When the enemy comes at you with condemnation and guilt over some past sin, go to your secret closet of prayer. Then place yourself in the awesome scene that took place in Israel.

Imagine yourself standing in the crowd, watching the two goats at the door of God's house. You see one goat being led inside to be sacrificed. Then you see the high priest laying his hands on the head of the other goat. You listen as the priest confesses your sins over the scapegoat.

Picture the able-bodied man leading the goat away. Watch as they cross beyond the borders of the camp and slowly disappear. Then, as they fade from view, shout, "There go my sins! There go my sins!" Let the truth sink in: "My sins are gone forever. They can never be used against me again. And they can never come back to haunt me. The Lord has removed them from my life forever."

The lamb of God has taken all of your sins upon

himself. And his sacrifice for you is good once and for all:

"Neither by the blood of goats and calves, but by his own blood he entered in once into the holy place, having obtained eternal redemption for us. For if the blood of bulls and of goats, and the ashes of an heifer sprinkling the unclean, sanctifieth to the purifying of the flesh: how much more shall the blood of Christ, who through the eternal Spirit offered himself without spot to God, purge your conscience from dead works to serve the living God?" (Hebrews 9:12-14).

2. God's call to repentance is proof there is forgiveness in his name.

Why the call for repentance? It is a revelation of God's forgiveness. After all, what good is repentance without the hope of forgiveness?

Think about it: what kind of God would our Lord be if he commanded a sinful people to humble themselves and repent, but then he left them waiting at the altar? If the Lord calls us to repent, when there is no way out for us – no deliverance from our guilt and shame – he wouldn't be a just, loving God. The very repentance to which he calls us infers forgiveness; indeed, it insists upon it. Wherever there is repentance, forgiveness has to be found. Therefore, his call for us to repent is proof that he forgives. Otherwise, the gospel would be a lie.

We have to believe that God forgives us when we repent. In fact, no repentance is acceptable to him unless it's accompanied by faith in his forgiveness.

Amazingly, many Christians have confessed their sins yet have never received the understanding of forgiveness. Oh, they've been convicted of their sins; they've confessed them, wept over them, been sorry for committing them. They've asked God to deliver them from their sins, and in some cases they've even made restitution for them. Yet they've never received a sense of God's pardon for their iniquity.

We see many examples of this in scripture. I think of Cain, Pharaoh and Ahab, to name just a few. And of course, there is Judas. The Bible says that after Judas betrayed Christ, he "repented himself" (Matthew 27:3). This man showed all the signs of heartfelt repentance. He confessed: "I have sinned" (27:4). He named his sin: "I have betrayed the innocent blood" (27:4). He even made restitution, returning the thirty pieces of silver he'd accepted for betraying the Lord (see 27:3). Why, then, didn't Judas' repentance bring him peace? Scripture tells us that immediately after Judas did these things, he "went and hanged himself" (27:5).

What was missing in Judas' repentance? It was this: Judas believed his sin was too grievous to be forgiven. He simply couldn't believe that a vile sin like his own could ever be pardoned. In short, he didn't have true faith in God's forgiveness. Judas' act of suicide stated, "My sin is too wicked, too hopeless ever to be forgiven." He couldn't accept the thought that he could ever be pardoned for betraying Christ. So he took his own life.

Likewise today, multitudes of sinners hang themselves on a tree of hopelessness. They go through the motions of life, but they've already given up hope. They may repent with tears. They may be truly sorry for their sin, naming and confessing every transgression, even making restitution as far as is humanly possible. But if they haven't trusted in God's forgiveness, all their acts of repentance are in vain.

You may think you can't be forgiven because of the awfulness of your sin. You're convinced your trespasses have been too deep and depraved for God to pardon. Yet I have already established to you that God's call for us to repent is proof he forgives. He cannot deceive.

You may answer, "But you don't know the depths of the sin I've committed. If you only knew the things I've done in secret. You know nothing about my hardness, my rebellion, my wicked thoughts. And you can't imagine the kind of blasphemy I've committed. I do things that are unnatural, contemptible, unholy. My heart is filthy. And I fall back into my sin often. There's no use in my even trying to approach God for forgiveness. I'm too far gone."

Try telling that to the apostle Paul. This man confessed he'd been a blasphemer, the chief of all sinners (see I Timothy 1:13, 15). The Bible is filled with further proof that God has forgiven the worst of sinners:

- "Know ye not that the unrighteous shall not inherit the kingdom of God? Be not deceived: neither fornicators, nor idolaters, nor adulterers, nor effeminate, nor abusers of themselves with

mankind, nor thieves, nor covetous, nor drunkards, nor revilers, nor extortioners, shall inherit
the kingdom of God. And such were some of you:
but ye are washed, but ye are sanctified, but ye
are justified in the name of the Lord Jesus, and by
the Spirit of our God" (1 Corinthians 6:9-11).

- Let the wicked forsake his way, and the unrighteous man his thoughts: and let him return unto
the Lord, and he will have mercy upon him; and
to our God, for he will abundantly pardon"
(Isaiah 55:7).

These passages also apply to the believer who has
fallen back into a grievous sin. Such a person finds
himself thinking, "I knew better than to do this. I
had been so convicted. And I'd made so many
promises to God. But now I've fallen back again.
And this time, it seems to be one fall too many.
There's no way God could forgive me for sinning
against the light as I have. I can't help thinking I've
sinned against the Holy Ghost. I've grieved him so
many times. How could God possibly forgive me
now, after I've done this over and over?"

Beloved, go back to God's word. Forsake your
sinful way. Return to the Lord in repentance. And
believe he will pardon you abundantly once again.
If you've read the passages above, yet you're still
unwilling to believe your sin can be forgiven, then
you're faking your grief. You simply want an excuse
to stay in your sins.

I say to every homosexual, every lesbian, every
transvestite, every sadomasochist, every rapist,

every child molester, even the worst of sinners: God doesn't give up on sinners. His word says he isn't willing for anyone to perish, not one person. And he calls you to repentance. He wants you to know him by his name – the God who pardons – because he wants to heal you and set you free.

So, don't say, "My sin is too powerful." Don't run from the Lord. And don't dare do as Judas did. Don't go out and hang yourself on some dead tree of hopelessness. Jesus himself says, "Wherefore I say unto you, All manner of sin and blasphemy shall be forgiven unto men ..." (Matthew 12:31).

Years ago, I almost gave up hope for homosexuals and others who struggle with sexual perversions. Our ministry had started a home for homosexuals, but it ended up becoming a nest of iniquity. Even the director, who was supposedly delivered from his homosexuality, turned back to his old lifestyle. Eventually, we had to shut down the home.

At the time, I thought, "This kind of ministry is hopeless." But over the years I've met more and more homosexuals, lesbians and others who once were bound but now have found freedom in Christ. At one time, they thought the only thing they could do was to come out of the closet and give themselves over to their sin. They let the devil convince them there was no hope for their lives, no victory available to them. But God never gave up on them. He found them in their sinful state, and he assured them, "There is hope for you. The blood of Jesus Christ has power to cleanse you."

You may be disheartened by certain Old

Testament warnings, such as, "(God) will laugh at your calamity; (he) will mock when your fear cometh" (Proverbs 1:26). You have to understand, these passages are written only to those who mock and refuse God's call to repentance. Some people have turned their backs on his offer of forgiveness and restoration. But if your heart is still open to God's voice, he won't reject you. The Lord will hear your cry.

Moreover, God's pardon has a supernatural effect. When you come to him in true repentance, believing he'll forgive you, he will fill your heart with a love for him and a hatred for sin. You'll never want to go back to your habit again. At times you may be tempted by it, but God's forgiveness will build strength into you, day by day.

Perhaps you've come to a place where you've accepted these terms of forgiveness. Yet now you're plagued by a fear: "I'm afraid if I ask God to forgive me, I'll go straight back to my sin." That fear has been put in you by the enemy. Above all, Satan wants to keep you from receiving the father's forgiveness. But your role is to go to the father, regardless. He'll give you the strength to deal with each temptation as it comes. You only need to face one day at a time. Jesus told us, "Sufficient unto the day is the evil thereof" (Matthew 6:34).

So, deal with your sin. Repent and accept God's forgiveness, right now. Say to yourself, "I'm forgiven today. And the Lord who has kept me today is going to keep me tomorrow, too. Day by day, he's going to add to me all the strength I need."

3. If God offers his forgiveness to sinners – thieves, drunkards, the covetous – how much more will he offer his forgiveness to his children who fall into sin?

The Lord has revealed himself to the ungodly as a God who pardons. Why would he deny the same revelation of himself to his own children?

Perhaps you love Jesus, yet you're troubled in heart. You're under a heavy weight of guilt, because you've fallen into a particular sin. You may be so cast down, you're not even able to look up. Once again, you've done the very thing you hate, and you've grieved the Holy Spirit. So now there's a breach between you and the Lord. Your sweet communion with him has become clouded.

You may know many Christians who are like you. They also trusted in God's forgiveness at one time, when they first came to Christ. But now that they've sinned horribly as believers, they find it hard, even impossible, to believe God will forgive them. Some have lived for years in fear and dread, always afraid the Lord is mad at them. Since their first year of walking with Jesus, they've never enjoyed the peace, joy and gladness that comes from trusting in his pardon and mercy.

Yet God offers us terms of reconciliation that he didn't even offer fallen angels. Those creatures had been holy, pure, obedient worshippers of God. But they fell into sin, and they weren't offered any way of escape. Instead, scripture says, "God spared not the angels that sinned, but cast them down to hell, and delivered them into chains of darkness, to be reserved unto judgment" (2 Peter 2:4).

The same is true for everyone who has died in sin. There are no terms of reconciliation for the dead. Try to imagine the fright of a sinner who has just died in the past hour. He already knows he faces damnation for all of eternity. How quickly he would jump at the chance to have God's forgiveness now. But his time is past. Now he can only await his dreaded judgment.

Yet to all who know the Lord, our God not only offers terms of reconciliation; he seeks to give us full forgiveness and peace. What amazing grace! The same Lord against whom we've sinned – whose commandments we've broken, whose name we've dishonored, whose love we've trampled – comes to us in mercy, urging us to be reconciled. He tells us, I want you back in sweet communion with me. And I want you once again to enjoy peace, gladness and rest in your soul. So, here are my terms: return to me, and believe in my forgiveness.

"No matter what your sin, no matter how cast down you are or guilt-ridden you feel, you can return to me in a moment's time. And you will enjoy my merciful pardon: full, free forgiveness. Your condition is not hopeless. So you needn't wallow in fear or dread for another hour. I'm offering you these simple terms of reconciliation, if you're willing to accept them."

Our flesh wants to get back into God's favor on its own terms.

We may know and accept God's terms of reconciliation. But our flesh can still want to make payment for our sins somehow, to try to pacify God's anger. It cries out, "How should I come before the Lord to be reconciled? Should I bow before him? Should I offer him sacrifices of some kind? How can I do penance? Can I pay for my sin with great self-denial? What can I do to appease God's anger with me?"

We see this attitude in Naaman, a captain in the Lord's army. At one point, Naaman contracted leprosy. When this devout man ran out of all medical hope, God told him he could still be healed. The Lord's only term, his one condition, was this: "Go and wash in Jordan ... and thou shalt be clean" (2 Kings 5: 10).

These weren't terms Naaman wanted to hear. Scripture says this godly man became angry "and went away in a rage" (5:12). Naaman was saying, in essence, "I don't like God's terms. How could this be so simple? I've been deceived somehow. I want my own terms."

But Naaman's servants challenged him, saying, "If God had told you to do some great thing, you would have done it in a heartbeat. You wouldn't hesitate to do something big, something sacrificial, something powerful in the strength of your flesh. But now God tells you to do one simple thing to receive your healing, and you refuse" (see 5:13).

Many Christians today are like Naaman. They've

set their own terms for their healing and cleansing. They don't want to come to the Lord on his simple, uncomplicated terms. They won't accept that they're merely to repent, return to the Lord and believe him for forgiveness. Instead, they think, "I've sinned so badly, I can't believe I'm supposed to just come to God and repent."

Like Naaman, we're convinced God needs some great thing from us before we can be cleansed and forgiven. So we tell ourselves we need to offer weeks of mortification, rivers of tears, days of fasting, nonstop witnessing, giving to the poor, reading the Bible all the way through several times. Or, we think, "I need to spend a few months grieving, sorrowing, weeping before I can even seek God's forgiveness and pardon. I've got to cry until God knows I'm sorry. How else will he know I'm grieved over what I've done?"

We think such terms are the only way we can ever compensate for our failure. But God has set the only acceptable terms. And those terms are simple and uncomplicated. His word tells us, "Thus saith the Lord God, the Holy One of Israel; In returning and rest shall ye be saved; in quietness and in confidence shall be your strength" (Isaiah 30:15).

By repenting, we return to God's rest. But first we have to believe in his forgiveness. This verse in Isaiah tells us, "In confidence shall be your strength," meaning, we have to be confident in God's readiness to forgive. We must be able to say confidently, "My God has forgiven me. I'm cleansed, healed, set free – all because he has wiped away my sins forever."

Most Christians reading this have heard these things hundreds of times before. So, why don't more of us quickly return to the Lord? Why don't we immediately throw ourselves on his mercy, lay hold of the New Covenant, and trust in his promise of Holy Ghost power to overcome sin's dominion? It's because we don't truly trust in his name – the God who pardons.

"They that know thy name will put their trust in thee: for thou, Lord, hast not forsaken them that seek thee" (Psalm 9:10). He will never forsake you. If you return to him, he'll reveal himself to you as the God who forgives.

Jesus told us he came "in my Father's name" (John 5:43). We know the father's name is forgiveness – the God who pardons. So, run to Jesus now, and receive God's mercy and forgiveness, in faith. His pardon in your life depends on your belief in his name – the God who forgives.

11

Christ Our Intercessor

"Wherefore he is able also to save them to the uttermost that come unto God by him, seeing he ever liveth to make intercession for them" (Hebrews 7:25).

What does scripture mean when it says Jesus makes intercession for us? I believe this subject is so deep, majestic and beyond human understanding, I tremble even to address it. Biblical scholars hold various views on its meaning. But no book or commentary has begun to satisfy my search. In fact, the more teaching I read on the matter, the more confusing it all sounds.

Yet, through prayer and trust in the Holy Spirit's guidance, I'm beginning to grasp just a little of this incredible subject. Recently, I've prayed very simply, "Lord, how does your intercession in heaven affect my life? Your word says you appear before the father on my behalf. What does this mean in my daily walk with you? I don't need to know what the great scholars have learned, just show me a simple truth I can grasp and appropriate for my life."

The English word intercession means to plead on another's behalf. This speaks of a figure who takes your place before others to plead your cause. When you hear such a definition – that is, an intercessor as someone who pleads for you – do you picture Christ continually pleading to God for you, asking for mercy, forgiveness, grace and blessings? In my opinion, this image makes our heavenly father appear tight-fisted. I simply refuse to believe that grace has to be pried out of our loving God. If we limit ourselves to such a narrow definition of inter-cession, we'll never understand the deeper spiritual meaning of what Christ does for us.

The Bible declares that my heavenly father knows my needs before I can ask him. And often, he supplies those needs even before I pray. Therefore, I find it difficult to accept that God's own son has to plead with him for anything. Besides, scripture says the father has already entrusted his son with all things: "In him dwelleth all the fullness of the Godhead bodily" (Colossians 2:9).

The popular evangelical view of Christ's interces-sion is that Jesus returned to heaven to act as high priest on our behalf. There is no question about this. The Bible clearly states: "Christ is not entered into the holy places made with hands, which are the figures of the true; but into heaven itself, now to appear in the presence of God for us" (Hebrews 9:24). "Christ being come an high priest of good things to come" (9:11).

I believe Jesus intercedes today to preserve his people, keeping us from sin and maintaining us in God's love. He won't allow anything – any fear, any temporary fall, any accusation from Satan – to alienate us from the father. In short, he prays for us in the same way he prayed for his disciple Peter: "that thy faith fail not" (Luke 22:32).

Some scholars believe Christ's mere presence in heaven is a kind of silent intercession. In other words, Jesus has already paid the price for our sin, shedding his own blood. Therefore, his nail-scarred hands and feet are a perpetual testimony of what he has accomplished on our behalf.

I have no problem accepting this picture of Christ's intercession. I've always found it hard to believe that every time I sin or face Satan's accusations, Jesus constantly has to appear before the throne to remind God of his sacrifice. This reflects the Old Testament system, when blood offerings had to be made for sin regularly. It also echoes the annual atonement sacrifice. That offering had to be made year after year, when the high priest carried blood and incense into the holy of holies to atone for the people's sin.

No, Jesus' sacrifice for us was made once and for all: "Nor yet that he should offer himself often, as the high priest entereth into the holy place every year with blood of others; for then must he often have suffered since the foundation of the world: but now once in the end of the world hath he appeared to put away sin by the sacrifice of himself" (Hebrews 9:25-26).

Note the phrase "but now once." This settles the matter. When Christ's blood was presented in heaven, it ended the need for any further sacrifice. His blood paid the price for all sin, for all time. And our heavenly father doesn't have to be constantly reminded of that fact.

Some Puritan scholars hold yet another belief about Jesus' intercession. They claim it has to do with the way Christ presents our prayers to the father. They quote this passage: "There was given unto him much incense, that he should offer it with the prayers of all saints upon the golden altar which was before the throne. And the smoke of the incense, which came with the prayers of the saints, ascended up before God out of the angel's hand" (Revelation 8:3-4).

This suggests that Jesus "perfumes" our prayers, or "filters" them, to make them acceptable to the father. In this way, he intercedes for us – or, mediates our prayers – before God's throne.

I agree that Christ adds his own incense to our prayers, but not to make them acceptable. This is where I have a theological problem. Scripture makes it clear that Jesus' sacrifice has already given us full access to the father. First, his work on the cross reconciled us to God. There, he opened to us the holy of holies. Now we are one in Christ; we simply can't be separated from him. We are bone of his bone, flesh of his flesh. And his presence in heaven has given us the right to go directly to the mercy seat. In this way, we have direct access to the heavenly father. Jesus himself said, "In that day ye shall ask me nothing. Verily, verily, I say unto you, Whatsoever ye shall ask the Father in my name, he will give it to you" (John 16:23).

Make no mistake, Jesus is our mediator. But he has

already done his work of mediation, on the cross.
Through his shed blood, he has reconciled us to
God. Now nothing stands between us and the
father's throne. This is one of the glorious victories
Christ won for us at the cross.

I don't claim to know everything about Christ's
intercession for us. But I do believe that whatever
our high priest is doing in his intercession for us, it
is a very simple matter. And I believe that intercession has to do directly with the growth of his body
here on earth. He is at work supplying every joint
and part with might and strength.

After much prayer, careful study and reliance on
the Holy Spirit, I have concluded this about Christ's
intercession for us:

**Jesus died on the cross to purchase peace with
God for me – and he's in heaven now to
maintain that peace, for me and in me.**

The peace we have with God through Christ
distinguishes our faith from all other religions.
Hindus worship thousands of gods. Muslims
worship Allah. But in both the Hindu and Muslim
worlds, there is no peace. Why? These gods are
powerless to pardon sin. According to their
beliefs, people have to work and strive, hoping
and praying they'll somehow be relieved of their
sins.

In every other religion besides Christianity, the sin
question is never settled. Sin's dominion simply
hasn't been broken. Therefore, there can be no

peace: "There is no peace, saith the Lord, unto the wicked" (Isaiah 48:22).

But we have a God who provides peace by pardoning sin. "I am the Lord thy God which teacheth thee to profit, which leadeth thee by the way that thou shouldest go. O that thou hadst hearkened to my commandments! Then had thy peace been as a river, and thy righteousness as the waves of the sea" (48:17-18).

This is the very reason Jesus came to earth: to bring peace to troubled, fearful humankind. He testified, "These things I have spoken unto you, that in me ye might have peace" (John 16:33). Before he ascended to heaven, he said, "Peace I leave with you, my peace I give unto you: not as the world giveth, give I unto you. Let not your heart be troubled, neither let it be afraid" (14:27).

How does Jesus maintain God's peace for me? He does it in three ways:

- First, Christ's blood removed the guilt of my sin. In this sense, Paul says, "He is our peace" (Ephesians 2:14). Jesus made peace for me through his blood. And now I no longer have to tremble in fear at the devil's accusations. Instead, I know I have a heavenly father who forgives and pardons my sin. He invites me to come boldly to his throne of grace, to receive his mercy. "We have access by faith into this grace wherein we stand" (Romans 5:2).
- Second, Christ maintains my peace and joy in believing: "Now the God of hope fill you with all

joy and peace in believing, that ye may abound in hope, through the power of the Holy Ghost" (Romans 15:13). "Therefore being justified by faith, we have peace with God through our Lord Jesus Christ" (5: 1). We have a God who forgives and pardons. And because of this, we can experience the joy and victory of having peace with the Lord.

- Third, Jesus causes me to rejoice at the hope of entering glory: "We ... rejoice in the hope of the glory of God" (Romans 5:2). "Having made peace through the blood of his cross, by him to reconcile all things unto himself" (Colossians 1:20). "And you, that were sometime alienated and enemies in your mind by wicked works, yet now hath he reconciled in the body of his flesh through death, to present you holy and unblameable and unreproveable in his sight" (1:21-22).

Simply put, peace is the absence of fear. And a life without fear is a life full of peace.

God promised us this kind of peace in the oath he made to Abraham. The Lord pledged to send a redeemer to his people, to deliver them from all enemy powers. This redeemer would enable us to live holy and without fear, all the days of our lives (see Luke 1:69-75).

Christ spent his years on earth preaching about and offering the peace of God. And he gave God's peace freely to all who received him. Peter says Christ "multiplies peace" to us: "Grace and peace be multiplied unto you through the knowledge of God, and of Jesus our Lord" (2 Peter 1:2). Today, all who name Jesus as their Lord have received his divine peace – peace with God and peace within.

Moreover, when Jesus ascended to heaven, he didn't just bask in the glory that God bestowed on him. He didn't take his place of power at the father's right hand merely to exult in his triumph. No, he went to the father to maintain the hard-won peace he achieved for us at Calvary.

Multitudes of Christians do not live by this truth. They live in terror, always upset, worried about their salvation, letting their conscience condemn them. But scripture says, "He ever liveth to make intercession for them" (Hebrews 7:25).

Our saviour is alive in glory right now. And he's both fully God and fully human, with hands, feet, eyes, hair. He also has the nail scars on his hands and feet, the wound in his side. He has never discarded his humanity; he's still a man in glory. And right now, our man in eternity is working to make sure we're never robbed of the peace he gave us when he left. He's ministering as our high priest, actively involved in keeping his body on earth full of his peace. And when he comes again, he wants us to "be found of him in peace" (2 Peter 3:14).

Two things threaten my peace with God: my conscience, and Satan's accusations, both in heaven and to me personally.

When I sin, my peace is interrupted in two areas.

First, my conscience troubles and accuses me, and rightly so. But, second, Satan's accusations put fear in me. I believe these are the two primary areas where Christ's intercession applies to us.

First, my high priest won't permit my conscience to hold me captive. As we saw in the previous chapter, he interdicts the conscience's condemning power. Nor will he allow Satan's accusations against me to go unchallenged. Christ is my advocate with the father against every accusation from hell.

Yet, what exactly is an advocate? It's simply "my friend in court." For Christians, this friend in court is also the son of the judge. In addition, our advocate is our brother. In fact, we're set to inherit the judge's fortune along with him. Does this mean the judge is my father as well? Yes, he is, by adoption.

So, this judge isn't adversarial with me at all. The truth is, he loves me as much as he loves his own son. He's clearly not on the plaintiff's side, but on mine.

Don't misunderstand, however; this isn't a rigged court. Although I'm related to the judge, he is absolutely just and holy, without exception. Suppose there is enough evidence stacked against the accused to send him to the electric chair. The judge can't just say, "This man seems awfully sorry. I know there's a lot of evidence against him, but I can't help feeling deeply for him. He cries a lot. And besides, I hate to see his family suffering through this trial. This is really painful to me. Suddenly, I feel merciful toward him. I've decided I'm going to dismiss all charges."

What judge anywhere would get away with this? Justice would be perverted.

In a recent poll, 82 per cent of Americans said they don't believe a person can get justice, unless he has a lot of money and a powerful team of lawyers. Apparently, people don't believe in justice anymore. But God still does. And he would never pervert his divine justice in this way. If he is eternally just, his justice has to be satisfied. And everything decided in his court must be according to divine justice. No human or devil can ever accuse him of showing favouritism. His justice will be meted out according to his divine law, with every debt paid in full.

It's important to note here that there are two courtrooms. The first court is in our hearts, where our conscience accuses us. The second court is in heaven, where Satan accuses us before the father. I believe Jesus' intercession takes place in both courts. Jesus the man in glory deals with Satan's accusations. And while the human Christ can't come down and deal with my conscience, his Spirit in me can. So, you see, Jesus' work for us can't be contained in either heaven or earth.

Christ's work of intercession for us includes something I've already mentioned: interdiction. This means to prohibit by placing under a legal sanction – or, in lay terms, to halt an action by a court order. It means getting a court order from a judge to stop someone's actions against you. Here's how I see interdiction working in our lives:

When we sin, we're breaking God's law. Of

course, God's laws are unchangeable. They're the beam of his glory, and he has to honour them. The Ten Commandments represent his moral law, and that law demands justice or payment. One of these laws states, "Thou shalt not commit adultery" (Exodus 20:14). Therefore, the law adds, "The adulterer and the adulteress shall surely be put to death" (Leviticus 20: 10).

You have to understand, we are not under the law as a means to salvation. In other words, we couldn't be saved by keeping the law perfectly. Rather, the law rules over our lives as boundaries of our behaviour. And if we cross those boundaries, we commit sin.

The law saves nobody but convicts everybody.

You can't fool your conscience. He's like a sheriff of the soul. He's been trained by God in the divine law, so he knows it well. And, as I stated previously, he abides by God's law without partiality. He has to arrest and charge every lawbreaker.

Of course, to law-abiding people, the conscience is no threat. But when you break the law, your soul-sheriff springs into action. God has commissioned him to handcuff you and bring you to prison. And he won't release you until the judge assures him justice has been served. It's nothing personal with the sheriff; he's just doing his job. He simply won't be prejudiced. He has to abide by the law.

The unrighteous person may try to bribe his

conscience. The Bible calls this searing the conscience (see 1 Timothy 4:2). This means rendering your conscience insensitive to the law, so that you excuse any legal violation. In this case, your conscience releases you without charging you. It simply overlooks your sin. Indeed, people who have seared their conscience "let themselves go" in regard to morality.

But if you're a godly person, your soul-sheriff can't be bought. He'll arrest you and show you how exceedingly serious your sin is. Then he'll remind you that the law always seeks a penalty of death.

Have you never been justly imprisoned by your conscience? Have you never felt the agony and pain of sinning against almighty God? Have you never been burdened by shame and sorrow because you've broken God's law, and now you must pay the penalty for it?

The job of our conscience is actually a wonderful work of God. He brings the law to us to show us the exceeding sinfulness of our sin. Otherwise, we would develop a hard heart.

My soul-sheriff has come to me on many occasions. No matter what my failure may be, he's there shouting, "Guilty, wicked, unholy." And he reminds me that I face God's wrath.

At the same time that my conscience arrests and imprisons me, Satan stands in the heavenlies accusing me. "The accuser of our brethren ... which accused them before our God day and night" (Revelation 12:10).

You may wonder why God would allow the devil to approach his throne with accusations against any of his children.

Why doesn't God simply ignore the charges that Satan brings against us? Speaking as a natural father, that's what I would do. I wouldn't tolerate anyone's gossip about my children. I would banish that person from my presence, saying, "I don't have to listen to your lies. Get lost."

But if someone knocks at my door and has a police officer with him, I'll be inclined to listen. You see, if my child's accuser can back up his accusations with legal charges, then they're no longer gossip. That officer is standing there for a reason. Now it's a legal matter.

This is how Satan operates. He can approach the Lord about us only in legal terms. And if his charges are true – if his accusations are based on actual guilt – then God must give him a hearing. (Of course, Satan had to falsify his charges against Jesus, who had no sin. But we are all guilty of sin, so the devil doesn't have to accuse us falsely.)

A number of years ago, an abortion clinic in New York City was picketed by a group of pro-life demonstrators. The clinic was located in a high-rise office building, and the building owners wanted them out. Finally, the owners succeeded in closing down the clinic for not paying a huge amount in back rent.

In anger, the clinic turned against Times Square Church, which also had offices in the building at the time. They sued our church, blaming us for hurting their business. They presented the judge with a long list of false charges, claiming I had rallied the pro-life demonstrators and that our church had sponsored them.

Because of this lawsuit, I had to give a deposition (a testimony under oath). I had to listen to all the charges and was asked to reply. But the case never went to trial. The judge threw it out, finding no evidence of guilt.

Likewise, Satan knows he can't come to God accusing us with trumped-up charges. He knows our righteous judge would never listen to spurious charges. And for two thousand years now, God hasn't listened to any unsubstantiated accusations against his children. What earthly judge would allow a lawyer to come back to his court time after time presenting only foolish accusations? Justice would be offended. And no judge would waste his time on such charges. So, do you think for a moment that God would allow the devil to come into his presence presenting only gossip against us? No. The Lord would throw him out immediately.

Satan cannot come to God's throne unless you are truly guilty. When he has a legal claim, he has a right to bring it to our father. And God is just; he will abide by his divine law. So, whenever the devil comes to the father to accuse you, it's because he has caught you breaking God's law. And before he comes to court, he makes sure he is informed on all the facts against you. He calls in all his demonic operatives to give him evidence against you.

In Revelation 12:10, the word accuser means plaintiff. This is a legal term for someone who brings up charges in court. Satan brings charges especially against those who are truly righteous in Christ. He sees this as his best chance to build a case against someone who's wholly surrendered to the Lord. So he makes sure he goes after the devoted one who has fallen into iniquity, sinning against the light.

You'd better believe Satan comes to God's court heavily armed with evidence. He carries in a well-documented dossier of facts to back up his charges. His demonic operatives recorded the very hour you sinned, the details of your indulgence, everyone involved, and the place where it happened. And you know it's all true. You're guilty of every undeniable fact.

Yet, God has allowed Satan to appear in his court for only one reason: he's going to shut the mouth of every demon and every human accuser. And he's going to procure his holy justice before the world, so he can never be accused of injustice (see Romans 3:19).

Here is where Christ's intercession has to be clearly understood.

The devil has brought his charges against you. He has piled up evidence upon evidence against you. And you're sitting in prison, crying and weeping, full of shame and guilt. So, what do you do now? You call your defense attorney, your advocate, your friend in court – Jesus.

When your advocate comes to you, he doesn't just pat you on the back and say, "It's okay. Everything's going to be all right. Don't worry, I'll take care of it." No – he looks you in the eye and says, "Before I can do anything for you, I have to hear from you: are you guilty? I know you're guilty, and the judge knows you're guilty. But do you know it? I can't go to court and present a case against your opponent unless the truth has been acknowledged. So, do you acknowledge your sin and repent?"

You tell your lawyer everything: "Yes, I'm guilty. I did it – I sinned. And I don't have any defense. I knew full well I was breaking the law. All this time, I've been living in fear, because I've known I'm condemned. I realize justice has to be done. And I know my penalty is death. Anything less wouldn't be just."

At that point, Jesus begins to intercede in the court of your heart. He must be persuaded you're sorry – that you're admitting your guilt and repenting. Then, Christ's Spirit begins to groan in you, making sounds so deep they can't be understood. This is the Spirit of Christ, praying to the father. "The Spirit also helpeth our infirmities: for we know not what we should pray as we ought: but the Spirit itself maketh intercession for us with groanings which cannot be uttered" (Romans 8:26).

I have experienced this kind of groaning in the Spirit. As a younger man, whenever I would sin, my conscience would bring shame and conviction upon me. I remember driving along once when suddenly I began weeping. I had to pull off the road. I thought, "Where is this coming from?" There was a groaning in my heart, a cry over sin by the Spirit that manifested in me as literal tears. I wept uncontrollably.

Even when it was over, I didn't understand it. But eventually I did. It was Jesus, my intercessor. He was groaning to the father, in a spiritual depth I knew nothing about: "I'm not letting David go. I'll bring him to repentance." This is a picture of Christ's amazing intercession, taking place right where I live, in my heart.

Have you experienced this? At one time, some sin of yours was simply too much to handle. You were in over your head, and you thought you were going down for good. Then Jesus' Spirit came to you and said, "I have to answer all the devil's charges." He began praying and interceding for you, groaning through you, telling the father, "Keep this one, Lord. Humble him. Break this power over him."

You know now it was your high priest, standing in his temple, interceding for you.

Now you are taken to court to stand trial.

Your judge, God, knows the charges against you are true. And your lawyer, Jesus, knows they're true. So your advocate doesn't bother to plead for you before the judge. Rather, he must interdict the plaintiff, Satan. It's up to your advocate to prove that your accuser has no case. His intercession in this court has to do with satisfying divine justice and with God's right to offer free pardon for your proven sins.

Jesus has his own evidence in hand. First, he has your repentance, your godly sorrow. And second, he has the indwelling of his own Holy Spirit in you, to keep you from going back to your iniquity.

The devil proceeds first. He names the charges, going straight to the law to point out what is written about your sin: "It's right here, God – adulterers must be put to death. And I have every proof against this man. You know full well what happened, God. You're omniscient. You can't deny I've got the goods on this person."

Now your lawyer turns to the judge. The father merely looks at his son as if to say, "Tell him what you've got."

Your advocate already knows this is strictly a legal matter. So he turns to the plaintiff, and he agrees with him. "Yes, my client is guilty," he says. "He's broken the law. I know more about it than you do, devil. So, if it's the law you want, Satan, I'll give you the law.

"You must know that the law makes provision for a substitutional atonement. After all, if one Adam could bring down guilt on all of humankind, a second Adam could bring salvation to all who believe.

"This law allowed for everyone's sins to be borne by a sacrificial animal. A goat was taken to the altar where it was sacrificed, its blood shed, its life taken, its body consumed. Meanwhile, another goat – or 'scapegoat' – was sent into the wilderness, bearing the people's sins. After that, the people's transgressions were gone forever. That was the law.

"But now the blood of a human substitute has been provided. And it has washed away the sins of all who trust in God. It is written, 'It pleased the Lord to bruise him; he hath put him to grief ... (and) made his soul an offering for sin ... and he bare the sin of many, and made intercession for the transgressors' (Isaiah 53:10, 12). Furthermore, it is written, 'By one offering he hath perfected for ever them that are sanctified' (Hebrews 10:14).

"Yes, God's law is holy and just. The lawbreaker must die for his sin. But, you see, Satan, a substitute has come to stand in for this guilty man before you. And that substitute has already paid the price for the man's sin. One has already paid the death penalty. So, the full demands of the law have been paid in full. This man is now guiltless. He's absolutely free."

At that point, your advocate holds up his hands for the plaintiff to see. He states, "On this proof I rest my case: these nail scars on my hands, the scars on my feet, the wound in my side. I'm the sacrifice, devil. You know I have paid all his debts. You have no case against my client."

Talk about an interdiction. Here we see the presence of a crucified man in glory, with marks on his body. This is the grand and glorious, voiceless intercession of Christ. And it ends all charges against you.

No more can be spoken against you now. You can shout, "My case is over, finished. Jesus' blood has blotted out all my transgressions. I'm a free man. The devil has nothing on me!"

Beloved, there is only one way we can regain our peace with God and maintain it. We must deal with the devil's accusations in legal terms. We can scream at Satan all day long, binding him, trampling him, ordering him around. But empty threats and human zeal have no power over him. He accuses us in legal terms, and we have to answer him likewise. So we must deal with him in a language he fully understands: he must be bound with truth.

God's word is the legal truth by which we silence Satan. It's the legal document that declares our innocence, and we're to stand on it at all times. After all, scripture was the legal language Jesus used to befuddle and defeat Satan during his wilderness temptation: "It is written ..." God's word remains the legal authority that sends the devil fleeing.

I know a wonderful Christian couple who were sued by hostile plaintiffs. Their case ended up being thrown out for lack of evidence. But that was only the beginning of the couple's problems. The plaintiffs started a campaign of harassment against them. They obtained legal letterhead and wrote threatening letters, saying, "It's not over. We're reopening the case and filing new charges. We're going to sue you for everything you've got."

At one point, a private detective began following the couple. They were terrified, overwhelmed, unable to sleep. Both husband and wife came close to having a nervous breakdown. Why? They'd forgotten about the legal document they were given when the case was thrown out. The judge had handed them their formal release, declaring them innocent of all charges. They could never be tried again on the same grounds. That was the law.

The same is true for you. Satan has lost his case against you. And you have the judge's document to prove it: God's word. Now the devil can't hurt you where it counts, before the judge's throne on Judgment Day. But you have to rely on God's word and trust in it. You must stand up to your accusers and read them your document of release.

Your soul-sheriff, the conscience, abides by the law. And because Christ has proven legally that you're free, you can show the sheriff your release document. When he sees you've been declared free, he'll move on to other work.

But the devil is another matter. He'll rage over his defeat, thinking, "I may have lost the case in court. But I'll win the battle in his mind." He'll harass and threaten you. He'll put a tail on you. He'll tell you God is mad at you. He'll trump up false charges in your mind and make you feel unworthy. He'll flood your mind with doubts, fears, lies from hell: "You're unclean. I don't care what anybody says. You know it in your heart."

That's when you have to go on the offensive. Turn to your legal document. Trust it, stand on it. Don't believe the devil's lies against you. Find the law of Christ, chapter and verse, and throw it in Satan's face: "When Jesus won my case, he gave me this legal document, devil. And it says: 'It is written …' I can't be tried for the same charges, ever again. So you can't accuse me with this same sin. The judge has thrown out those charges for good. It can't go back to court.

"Therefore, I live with the full assurance that my sins are forgiven. My sin question is settled forever."

Let no one – no devil, no human, no voice – rob you of the peace Christ has given you. "Who is he that condemneth? It is Christ that died, yea rather, that is risen again, who is even at the right hand of God, who also maketh intercession for us" (Romans 8:34).

Praise God for Christ's dual intercession – in the court of your heart, and in the court of heaven. Jesus has you covered on all fronts.

Hallowed be his names.

RHP One Pound Classics

DAVID WILKERSON
Hungry For More of Jesus
The way of intimacy with Christ
Hallowed Be Thy Names
Knowing God as you've never known Him before

ANDREW MURRAY
The True Vine
Fruitfulness and stability in Jesus

ROY HESSION
The Power of God's Grace
The way of peace, joy and genuine revival
We Would See Jesus
Finding in Jesus everything we need

OSWALD J SMITH
The Revival We Need
A heart-stirring cry for revival
The Enduement of Power
The power of the Holy Spirit in the Christian life

CHARLES FINNEY
Revival
God's way of revival

Please ask for these titles at your local
Christian bookshop

RHP One Pound Classics

The Power of God's Grace
by Roy Hession

The way of peace, joy and genuine revival

This powerful book is for Christians old and new. With his fresh portrayal of grace, Roy Hession shows how you really can experience joy, peace and revival in your Christian life.

Roy Hession says, *I have been seeking to proclaim the whole message of grace since I was confronted with revival in 1947. Though I was a full-time evangelist, I was profoundly moved by this confrontation with living revival and I began a new walk with the Lord. As a result, I was given a new concept of the gospel of the grace of God by means of which God accomplishes the revival of His church and the salvation of the lost. This book is the direct result of that new concept.*

(This book was previously published under the title *Good News for Bad People*)

Now available from your local Christian bookshop